Oil and Water

Two Faiths: One God

Amir Hussain

Oil and Water

Two Faiths: One God

CopperHouse

Editors: Byron Rempel-Burkholder and Michael Schwarzentruber
Cover and interior design: Margaret Kyle and Verena Velten
Proofreader: Heather Picotte
Cover art: Getty Images, adapted from Photodisc, *Symbols & Icons*

 CopperHouse is an imprint of Wood Lake Publishing, Inc.
Wood Lake Publishing acknowledges the financial support
of the Government of Canada. Nous reconnaissons l'appui financier du gouvernement
du Canada. Wood Lake Publishing acknowledges the financial support of the Province
of British Columbia through the Book Publishing Tax Credit.

At Wood Lake Publishing, we practise what we publish, being guided by a concern
for fairness, justice, and equal opportunity in all of our relationships with employees
and customers. Wood Lake Publishing is committed to caring for the environment
and all creation. Wood Lake Publishing recycles, reuses, and encourages readers to
do the same. Resources are printed on 100% post-consumer recycled paper and more
environmentally friendly groundwood papers (newsprint) whenever possible. A
percentage of all profit is donated to charitable organizations.

Library and Archives Canada Cataloguing in Publication
Hussain, Amir
Oil and water : two faiths : one God / Amir Hussain.
Includes bibliographical references and index.
ISBN 10: 1-896836-82-8
ISBN 13: 978-1-896836-82-9
1. Islam. 2. Islam--Relations--Christianity.
3. Christianity and other religions. I. Title.
BP161.3.H88 2006   297   C2006-903417-6

Published by CopperHouse
An imprint of Wood Lake Publishing, Inc.
485 Beaver Lake Road, Kelowna, BC, Canada, V4V 1S5
www.woodlake.com
250.766.2778

Printing 10 9 8 7 6
Printed in Canada

Table of Contents

Foreword

by Derek Evans[1]

When I was a young man, I did a university degree in comparative religion. At the time, none of my friends or relatives imagined that this could possibly be the basis for a career – or anything else useful or relevant in the real world for that matter. The study of religion was generally regarded almost as an arcane branch of archaeology – an examination of ancient mysteries that would gradually fade in the face of scientific technology, free market economics, and the Western cultural values that we have come to refer to as globalization. People took for granted that universal human rights were an accepted and progressive norm, which everyone throughout the world would increasingly support and enjoy. At the same time, they believed that the influence of religion in domestic politics and international relations would gradually decline and eventually disappear. The future, it was thought, would be characterized by some combination of freedom *of* religion and freedom *from* religion. Both trends were generally assumed to be good for the health and well-being of the human family, and both have turned out to be terribly wrong.

The deeper we step into the 21st century, the clearer it becomes that if we are to survive as a species, let alone become a healthy family, we must take seriously the reality and significance of the world's great spiritual traditions. We are challenged with the urgent need to discover constructive and creative ways of relating with each other in open, honest, and respectful relationships. Yet we seem increasingly caught in a complex dialectic of distrust and resentment that allows little room for dialogue, and that threatens to condemn us to a perpetual spiral of division and conflict. As the turmoil surrounding the Danish cartoons of the Prophet Muhammed began to subside, a headline in *The Economist* captured not only the difficulties of the moment, but the dynamic that has characterized much of the thousand-year relationship between the Islamic world and the Christian and humanist traditions of the West: "Mutual Incomprehension, Mutual Outrage."[2]

Although they may not legitimately reflect the beliefs or behaviours of most people in their communities, extremist and fundamentalist elements have assumed a pre-eminent role as leaders or representatives for many of the world religions during the past decade – at least in the eyes of the media and popular culture. These extremist forces tend to oppose dialogue and erect obstacles to understanding. Too often, they have combined with virulent nationalist or other ideological sentiments, resulting in repression and violence. We cannot escape our history – our only options are to blindly repeat it, or to create a new future by taking responsibility for understanding and building healthy relationships with those with whom we share this planet.

This is a generous and hopeful book. Amir Hussain offers us not only a helpful contribution to the task of creating a new future, but also a necessary challenge. In presenting an intimate and insightful perspective on his own faith, he invites each of us to honestly examine and engage with what is truly meaningful in our own traditions and commitments. Readers may not always agree with his views, and may sometimes find it difficult to grasp the purpose or value of some aspects of Islam, but *Oil and Water* is an invitation to an ongoing relationship of dialogue, a proposal that we accompany and "help each other to find what is meaningful in our own tradition." By opening a conversation that seeks to better understand where we have come from, Amir Hussain enables us to address the question of what we want to become – individually and together.

I believe that human rights (such as freedom of thought and expression) and healthy relationships (such as the ability to engage in genuine dialogue) are ultimately the only defense we have against extremists and ideologues, and the tyranny, intolerance, and fear that are their constant companions. Rights can be challenging and real dialogue can be tough. Rights demand that we commit to treating ourselves and each other with profound and passionate respect. Dialogue is not about being nice, or about pretending that we are all the same. It requires that we recognize our real differences; relate to each other constructively, even when we are in opposition; and stand in solidarity with each other when one of us is attacked. Most of all, it requires that we accept the fact that we both may be changed, even transformed, in the course of our dialogue.

The symbol of both the human rights movement and of interfaith dialogue is the candle – fire for giving light, not for burning. With *Oil and Water*, Amir Hussain has gifted us with an offering of light.

Preface

I write these words during Lent, the period leading up to Easter, the most important religious holiday for Christians. For years, part of my Lenten routine has been to read the Gospel of Mark, considered by scholars to be the earliest of the New Testament accounts of Jesus' life. This year, I am reading Steve Ross' *Marked*, a retelling of the Gospel as a graphic novel (what comic books become when adults read them).

Yet I am a Muslim. Lent and Easter are important to me because the relationships between Islam and Christianity and between Muslims and Christians are also important to me. Those relationships are at the heart of this book.

I am a Western Muslim. For readers who think this is an oxymoron, I hope this book will gently disabuse them of the notion that Muslims cannot be Western. I was born in Pakistan, and moved with my family to Canada when I was four years old. All of my education, from kindergarten to PhD, was in Toronto and its suburb of Oakville, Ontario.

In 1997, I moved to southern California, where I have been teaching ever since. Currently, I am an associate professor in the Department of Theological Studies at Loyola Marymount University, the Jesuit university in Los Angeles. It is here, in this Catholic setting, that this book was written, and so my first thanks go to Loyola Marymount University for supporting me in writing this book.

As a Muslim growing up in Canada of the 1970s, I understood very early what it means to be a minority. Minority people have to know about the majority in order to survive, but the majority does not have to learn about the minority. Since

Christianity is the dominant religious tradition in Canada, I learned a lot about Christianity. The school year was based on the Christian calendar, with no classes on Sunday or during the Christmas break. At school, I said the Lord's Prayer daily as part of opening exercises, performed in the Christmas (not "holiday") pageant, and learned Christmas carols in music class.

Today, as part of a Canadian community living in the United States, I experience minority issues differently. My adopted country is the world's only "hyper-power," unmatched in its combination of military, economic, and cultural might. While most Canadians live a short distance away from the U.S. border and know a great deal about their neighbours, Americans tend to know very little about Canada. I am therefore seen as a foreigner from Canada more than I am seen as a Muslim. As a Canadian I experience being an immigrant all over again.

A quest for understanding: pleas and acknowledgements

This book is written for people who want to learn more about Islam and Muslims, particularly as they relate to Christianity and Christians. For many people, Islam has become synonymous with violence, especially after the horrible terrorist attacks in America on September 11, 2001, in Madrid on March 11, 2004, and in London on July 7, 2005. Many think that the Qur'an, the holy book of Islam, is a book of violence – or at least that it is much more violent than the Bible. A number of important Christian leaders have made very negative comments about Islam that only reinforce this notion. They see Islam as a threat to the values of the "Christian West." Like oil and water, they do not mix. As a Muslim, I am deeply concerned about violence committed by Muslims, especially when it is done in the name of Islam. However, as a Muslim, I also see the truth and beauty in my religion, and I choose to remain Muslim. As someone who loves to eat and cook, I know that oil and water can often be combined to produce delicious results. I see oil and water as necessary ingredients, not as mutually exclusive categories, which is why I have used them for my title.

I bring a number of unique gifts to this book. My PhD is from the University of Toronto's Centre for the Study of Religion, where I wrote my dissertation on Muslim communities in Toronto. I studied Christianity in my graduate years, and have been teaching courses in world religions for over a decade, at universities across Canada and the United States. I have been involved in interfaith work for over two decades. My late wife Shannon L. Hamm, who died in 1992, was a member of the United Church of Canada. Shannon's father came from a Mennonite background in Manitoba, so I am particularly pleased that my editor, Byron Rempel-Burkholder, is also Mennonite.

I have taught for several years at the Naramata Centre, a retreat centre of the United Church in the Okanagan Valley of British Columbia. This book has its roots in a course I taught there in 2004, when one of the participants, Bonnie Schlosser, asked me to think about writing something for Wood Lake Publishing. For this project, I worked most closely with Mike Schwartzentruber at WoodLake. The Executive Director of the Naramata Centre in 2004 was Derek Evans, who graciously agreed to write the foreword for this book. A number of other people whom I first met at Naramata have also influenced this book: the Thompson-Goodchild family (Jim, Cyndi, Miriam, and Sarah), the Strathdee family (Jim, Jean, Michael, and Julie), Darryl and Jeryl Auten, Jean and Robyn Pelletier, Linnea Good, Diane Ransom, Allison Rennie, Pat Deacon, Nick Stebbing, and Bill Horne.

While I remain a Muslim, I have strong connections to the United Church of Canada and less formal associations with the United Methodist Church in the United States. When I am in Toronto, I try to attend worship services at Trinity-St. Paul's United Church. There is something about this church that fills a spiritual need for me. In 2004 I asked to become an adherent, a membership category that would allow me to formally associate with the congregation, but without converting. I am truly grateful to Trinity-St. Paul, particularly pastors Hal and Karen Llewellyn, and parishioners Joan and Peter Wyatt, Roger and Moira Hutchinson, and Michael Cooke and Juliet Huntly (as well as their children).

I owe a special acknowledgement to Paul Newman and Bruce Gergersen for their interfaith work in the United Church. I have also been privileged to learn from three former moderators of the United Church, Bruce McLeod, Lois Wilson, and Stan McKay. In the United Methodist Church of the United States, I am indebted to Jim and Margaret Allen, Ken Ellis, James Lawson, Jim and Amy Goss, and Don and Rose Sparling. Other Christian friends who have been deeply influential on my understandings of both Islam and Christianity include Rick and Anne Talbott, Crerar and Roxanna Douglas, Chad Hillier, Michael LeVan, Randal Cummings, Caroline Lapp, Howard Happ, and Pat Nichelson. To all of these church friends, I am profoundly thankful. They have exemplified an important truth about interfaith dialogue: It works best not when we try to convert each other, but when we help each other to find meaning in our own traditions.

I have also done interfaith work with various Jewish communities in North America. In many ways, Judaism and Islam have more in common with each other than either one does with Christianity. However, it would take a separate book to compare all three religions. For that reason, while I mention Judaism throughout this book, the main comparisons will be between Islam and Christianity.

Finally, I need to acknowledge my own teachers, who are many. They include Peter Richardson, Bill Klassen, Michel Desjardins, Stephen Wilson, Jerry and Beth Bentley, Glenn Loney, Douglas Freake, Cynthia and Michael Desrochers, Edda Spielmann, Fred Denny, Jane McAuliffe, Glenn Yocum, Emelie Olson, Michael Sells, William Chittick, Sachiko Murata, Jack Miles, Tazim and Zayn Kassam, Farid Esack, Ahmet Karamustafa, Ebrahim Moosa, Don Weibe, and Neil McMullin.

Confessions of a Muslim admirer of Christianity

I will eventually articulate some points of difference between Islam and Christianity. But at this point I want to confess how I appreciate Christianity, even though I am not a Christian. I honour Jesus as a prophet, and I believe in the literal truth of the virgin birth, an article of faith that some of my Christian friends do not accept (but that is another topic). I do not accept that Jesus is God, and I do not think that Jesus' death saves us from sin. Intellectually, I can't get my head around the ideas of God coming to earth in human form (the Incarnation), or of God dying for our sins.

However, when I sing the songs of Christian worship, I "get it" at a visceral level. There is something about the modern Christian songs of the Strathdees, Jim Manley, Gordon Light, Bruce Cockburn, Linnea Good, and Carolyn McDade that speaks to my soul. But I am also moved by older songs of praise, specifically those of Hank Williams and John R. Cash. When I sing Old Hank's "I Saw the Light" or "Jesus Died For Me," I understand what it means for Christians to think of Jesus as their Lord and Saviour. And when I hear Cash sing the hymns that he knew in childhood, I am moved beyond words. When I hear him sing "The Man in White" or read his book of the same name, I understand more about Paul spreading Christianity than I learn from reading a dozen scholarly articles on the topic.

For me, Christianity is a lived reality in which I can participate through song. It was in this way, through accidents of history and geography (accidents that religious people call "grace") that I first met Joan Becker when she was rehearsing with the choir of First United Methodist Church in North Hollywood. I had been invited to that church in November, 2001, to offer a reflection at a Thanksgiving service of an interfaith food pantry. Since then, Joan has been a part of my life, and it is to her that this book is dedicated.

Note on the sources and Qur'an translation in this book

In writing this book, I have drawn information from various sources that are sometimes cited in endnotes. The sources that I use are listed in the suggestions for further reading at the end, and readers interested in learning more about particular topics are referred there.

The version of the Qur'an that I have consulted throughout this book is Abdullah Yusuf Ali's English translation, which presents the Arabic text along with Ali's translation in parallel columns. As someone trained in the Arabic language, I begin with the Arabic original, and compare that with Ali's translation. I use inclusive language wherever possible, and certainly for the terms associated with God. Since this is not intended as a book for scholars, I simplify the translation and update some of the delightful but archaic English that Ali used, thus making the text as straightforward as possible for the beginning reader. Sometimes this requires the addition of words to make explicit in English what is implicit in the Arabic text. In my translation, I have been influenced by the work of Michael Sells and William Chittick, whom I consider to be the finest Qur'an translators in the English language. To both of them, I am profoundly thankful. Readers who wish to see other translations are referred to this web page, which gives the Ali translation alongside two other English versions: http://www.usc.edu/dept/MSA/quran

PART ONE

Introducing Muslims and Islam

1

After 9-11: Muslims in an uneasy limelight

The evening before the terrorist attacks of September 11, 2001, I had led a session for a world religions course on death and dying. Since it was only the second meeting of the course, I was still introducing students to the topic. I asked the students, "What object, film, song, piece of music, art, or writing helps you to understand death?" My own contribution to the discussion was Lou Reed's song, "Magic and Loss," from the CD of the same title, released in 1992. The CD and the title song were occasioned by the death of two of his closest friends. The song ends with the line, "There's a bit of magic in everything and then some loss to even things out." 1992 was also the year that my wife Shannon died suddenly and unexpectedly; the CD helped me in my own grieving. In my mind, Lou Reed was also synonymous with New York City.

Early the next morning, a friend phoned me, insisting that I turn on the television. I watched as the horrors of 9-11 unfolded. My first thoughts were about my friends in New

York, including an editor who lives a few blocks away from the World Trade Center. I went into the office to email friends whom I could not reach by telephone. It took me most of that terrible day to confirm that my friends were still alive. During that day our university provost contacted me to help put together a small committee to deal with the issues arising from these events. We cancelled classes that afternoon. The following day, I urged our provost to hold a memorial on our campus, which we did on Friday, September 14.

During that week, as it became clear that the group of hijackers responsible for the atrocities were Muslim, Muslims around the world condemned the attacks. For those of us in America, the attacks were against us; Muslims were included in the people who were murdered. The thoughts and prayers of American Muslims, like those of non-Muslims in America and around the world, were with the victims and their families, not with the terrorists. Internationally, Muslim leaders condemned the attacks in their Friday afternoon sermons on September 14.

Unfortunately, these condemnations were inadequately reported. Rev. Sandra Olewine, Jerusalem liaison for the United Methodist Church at the time, wrote home about a memorial service at Jerusalem's St. George's Anglican Cathedral: "When we left the cathedral after the service, we drove by the American Consulate in East Jerusalem. Gathered there were about 30 Palestinian Muslim schoolgirls with their teachers. Looking grief-stricken, they held their bouquets of dark flowers and stood behind their row of candles. Silently, they kept vigil outside our Consulate. But no cameras captured their quiet sorrow."

Not only were such events not reported; Muslims in general were still portrayed negatively in the media. Sadly, some religious leaders joined the fray, speaking of Islam as a dangerous religion, and Muslims as a violent people. The terrorists were taken to represent Islam instead of being seen for what they were: a dangerous lunatic fringe. As a result, many Muslims started doing interfaith work to educate others about Islam. At New York City's Cathedral of St. John the Divine, for example, Muslims helped to organize an interfaith memorial service that included visual art by a group of Muslim artists.

Prior to 9-11, I would give a presentation about Islam every two months or so. In the months afterwards, the frequency increased to every three days. During these presentations, I learned about some of the horrible misconceptions that people had about Islam and Muslims. Some thought that the Qur'an was a book of violence, and that Muslims were engaged in a bloody battle to kill non-Muslims. Yet almost everyone who came was seeking to understand this religious community that had been, until then, largely hidden from their consciousness.

The first interfaith event I spoke at after 9-11 was at the invitation of a Japanese American congregation of the United Methodist Church. Their own history included familiar parallels to the terrorist attacks, particularly Pearl Harbour during World War II, when Japanese Americans were placed in internment camps. Remembering this time when very few people stood with them, Japanese Americans have helped sponsor a number of interfaith and intercultural events that bring their communities together with Muslim Americans. At such events the gratitude of Muslim Americans for this support has been palpable.

Unfortunately, despite all these efforts, a great many hate crimes were nevertheless committed against Arabs, South Asians, and those whose ethnicity resembled that of the terrorists. On April 30, 2002, just seven months after the attacks, the Council on American-Islamic Relations (CAIR) released its seventh annual report on the status of Muslim civil rights in the United States. The report detailed 1,516 complaints that the CAIR received – a three-fold increase over the previous year. Some 2,250 people were affected by these complaints. Most troubling for the CAIR was that most of the complaints involved various levels of government: "Of all the institutional settings tracked by this report, the largest number of complaints involved profiling incidents at airports or those at the hands of government agencies, especially the INS [Immigration and Naturalization Service], the FBI, and local law enforcement authorities."

While the Patriot Act of October 26, 2001, and the passenger profiling at American airports did not target only Muslims, they nevertheless were worrisome to many North American Muslims. I had my own experience of ethnic targeting when I was fingerprinted and photographed while returning to the United States from Vancouver. But even that incident seems insignificant when seen against the estimated 1,200 Muslims who were detained, the 5,000 Muslim foreign nationals who were "voluntarily" interviewed, and the three Muslim charities (Holy Land Foundation for Relief and Development, Global Relief Foundation, and Benevolence International Foundation) that were closed by the federal government – all in the first year after 9-11.

Many American Muslims perceived that they were being targeted by their own government. This was particularly galling for the American Muslims who had voted for George W. Bush in the 2000 presidential election precisely because he had spoken out against the "secret evidence" that was often used against Muslims. Many sensed they did not have the basic human rights that were given to other Americans; while they considered themselves American and had all the rights of U.S. citizens, they felt they were not considered as such by their own government.

Since 9-11, more violence has erupted involving Muslims. First came the war in Afghanistan, followed in 2003 by the war in Iraq. 2004 saw the terrorist attacks in Spain, followed a year later by terrorist attacks in Britain. In 2005 and 2006 Muslims reacted, sometimes violently, to cartoons of the Prophet Muhammad published in a Danish newspaper (see Chapter Three). This list is by no means exhaustive, but it shows how some contemporary Muslims are caught up in cycles of violence. However, a far greater number of Muslims, especially those in North America, are living peaceful lives in harmony with their neighbours. Unfortunately, that does not elicit the same news coverage. As a Muslim, I lament this gap.

Other events involving Muslims were not violent, but were nevertheless troubling. One thinks, for example, of the debate in Ontario in 2004 and 2005 about the use of faith-based arbitration for family law in the Muslim immigrant community (see Chapter Seven). This was popularly misunderstood as Canadian Muslims seeking to impose *shari'ah* (Islamic religious law) in the Province of Ontario. Internationally, one might also recall the 2006 case of an Afghani man who was given a death sentence – which, thankfully, was later withdrawn – for his conversion to Christianity.

Unfortunately, trouble points like these have been present since the beginning of Islam 14 centuries ago. But they are part of a mixed picture of ups and downs in the way Muslims and Christians have related historically. Sometimes, the relationships have involved violence – the Crusades immediately come to mind. Other times, they have been characterized by toleration and admiration, as the "Golden Age" of medieval Spain illustrates. Sometimes, as in the Armenian genocide of 1915, Muslims have killed Christians. At other times, Christians have killed Muslims, as in the Srebrenica massacre of 1995, where more than 7,000 Bosnian Muslims were killed by Serbian Christians. Sometimes, as during Europe's "Dark Ages," Muslims have been dominant in civilization, making huge contributions to science, medicine, and mathematics. Other times, as during European expansionism and colonialism, Muslims have been in a subordinate position.

Some of this history is discussed in the next chapter, along with the changing demographics in North America. But before we get to that discussion, it may be helpful to address a few basic questions about who Muslims are and what they believe. I deal with these in greater detail throughout the remainder of the book, but for now, this might serve as an introduction.

What does *Islam* mean?

Islam is an Arabic word that means "submission" or "surrender." It can also mean "peace." Islam is therefore sometimes translated as "peaceful submission" or "engaged surrender." While the word *peace* has a positive connotation in the West, the words *submission* or *surrender* usually do not. All sorts of classes and workshops are available – and shy people are often encouraged to take them – that are designed to make people more assertive. We are taught in school and in sports to never surrender, to always keep fighting, even if we are losing. However, the surrender in Islam is not to any human person or authority, but to God. The best translation of the word *Islam*, therefore, is "a peaceful surrender to God." In this way, Islam as a concept should be familiar to those who also worship the one true God, especially Christians and Jews.

Islam is the name given to the world's second largest religious tradition, in terms of the number of adherents. Worldwide, more than one billion followers of Islam call themselves Muslims. In North America and Europe, there are more than 10 million Muslims; there are many more than this, of course, if we include Turkey as part of Europe. In countries such as Canada, France, Germany, and Britain, Islam is already the second largest religion behind Christianity. In the United States, some studies show that Islam is surpassing Judaism as the second largest religion.

Who is a Muslim?

The word *Muslim* comes from the word *Islam* and means "one who submits to God." Islam is therefore the name of the religious tradition, while a Muslim is a member of that tradition. Just as we have Christianity and Christians and Judaism and Jews, so we have Islam and Muslims. The term *Moslem* is the same word in Arabic, but *Muslim* is a more accurate transliteration into English. An even older word used in the West is *Mohammedans*. This is not a word that Muslims use for themselves; in fact, Muslims may take it as a term of derision. They consider themselves to be followers of God, and not worshippers of the Prophet Muhammad.

Who was Muhammad?

Like Judaism and Christianity, Islam is a prophetic religion; its followers believe God uses prophets to tell human beings how they are to live in the world. The prophet that is most associated with Islam is the Prophet Muhammad. His name is sometimes transliterated as "Mohammed", but "Muhammad" is more correct. Muhammad lived in the Arabian cities of Mecca and Medina from 570 to 632 CE. For Muslims, Muhammad is not the first prophet, nor the only prophet. But they believe Muhammad to be the final and most important prophet sent by God, because he brought God's final revelation to humanity.

What is the Qur'an?

Muslims believe that between the years 610 to 632 CE, God sent revelations to the Prophet Muhammad. These were collected into a book known as the Qur'an (*Koran* as it is less accurately transliterated). The word *Qur'an* means "recitation" or "reading." Muslims consider the Qur'an to be the very word of God, not a book written by the Prophet Muhammad. Roughly four-fifths as long as the New Testament, the Qur'an is the scripture for Muslims.

The original language of the revelation was Arabic. Since Muslims believe the Qur'an to be authored by God, only the Arabic original is referred to as the Qur'an, even though the Qur'an has been translated into every language used by Muslims. (Only about 20 percent of today's Muslims are native speakers of Arabic.) Since all translation involves human interpretation, the translations do not have the same status of revealed scripture that is given to the Arabic text.

What do Muslims have in common
with Christians and Jews?

In many ways, Muslims, Christians, and Jews hold much in common. All three religions are monotheistic, involving the worship of one God. This book assumes that they all worship the *same* God, even though each faith has different understandings of God. Some conservative Christians argue that Muslims and Christians worship different gods, since Christians believe that Jesus is God while Muslims do not. However, since Jews also do not believe that Jesus is God, but Christianity emerges out of a Jewish context, it becomes problematic for these same Christians to say that Jews and Christians worship different gods. Especially since monotheism is so important to all of our traditions, I prefer to speak of one God who has created us all and whom we all seek in our various ways.

In the Arabic language of the Qur'an, God is known as *Allah*, cognate with the Hebrew word for God, *eloh*, used in the Bible. To claim that Muslims do not worship God but Allah would be as absurd as saying that French speakers do not worship God but Dieu, or that Spanish speakers worship Dios. Indeed, Arabic translations of the New Testament – and about half of the Arabs in North America are Christians – refer to God as *Allah*.

The three religions are also prophetic traditions. The Qur'an mentions a number of prophets by name. Many of these are figures found in the Hebrew Bible, including Abraham, Jacob, David, Solomon, Moses, and others, even if Jews do not consider them all to be prophets in the usual sense. Indeed, the prophet that is mentioned most by name in the Qur'an is Moses. The Qur'an also mentions as prophets three New Testament figures: Zechariah, John the Baptist, and Jesus. Muslims believe that Jesus was a great prophet, born of the Virgin Mary who, interestingly, is mentioned more by name in the Qur'an than she is in the New Testament. However, Muslims do not believe that Jesus is divine, and they reject Christian notions of the Trinity.

What are the main differences between Islam, Judaism and Christianity?

The differences between the three religions emerge out of their unique histories. Judaism comes into the world first and establishes a covenant between God and the children of Abraham, the patriarch. This relationship is reinforced when Moses receives the Torah from God in the covenant at Sinai. Centuries later, a group of Jews breaks away, claiming that one particular Jew, Jesus, is the expected Messiah, the anointed one of the Lord. This group, which becomes the Christian church, sees itself in continuity with the earlier tradition. But this new community has a new covenant relationship to God through the person of Jesus. They also have a new text, the New Testament, which describes this new relationship. For Jews, there is nothing wrong with the "old" covenant, so they do not give credence to Jesus and the new texts about him. Some six centuries after Jesus comes Muhammad, with a tradition that sees itself in continuity with Judaism and Christianity. Again, there is a new prophet, Muhammad, and a new text, the Qur'an.

Jews, Christians, and Muslims all use different sacred texts. Jews consider the Hebrew Bible to be scripture. Christians incorporate the Hebrew Bible into the first part of their text, referring to it as the Old Testament, but they add a second collection of texts, the New Testament. The Hebrew Bible and the Old Testament are read very differently by Jews and Christians. Christians tend to read the Old Testament in light of the New Testament, using the New Testament as the lens through which to view the Old Testament. Muslims, for their part, have a different text altogether, the Qur'an. In the Qur'an, Jews and Christians are referred to as "People of the Book," indicating that they have their own revealed texts to follow.

Jews, Christians, and Muslims all emphasize prayer and worship, but these practices take different forms. Fasting is also shared by these three traditions, but it looks quite different in each tradition. Some of the dietary practices of Muslims – prohibitions against pork, or the ways in which animals are to be slaughtered for meat – are similar to the dietary practices of Jews. Muslims and some Christian groups prohibit alcohol, but most Jews and Christians do not.

Are all Muslims the same?

There are over a billion Muslims in the world, so any attempt to put them all into one box would be absurd. Just as Catholicism in England looks different from Catholicism in French Canada, or among Latino communities in Southern California, so Islam in Indonesia is unlike Islam in France. As in other religious traditions, some of the differences among Muslims are cultural. Muslims in Pakistan, for example, will break the Ramadan fast with samosas, while Muslims in Malaysia will break the fast with a rice dish.

Some differences are within the Muslim tradition itself. As we will see in the next chapter, there are two main branches of Islam, Sunni and Shi'a. The Sunni are the majority, making up about 85 percent of the Muslim world. The minority community, about 15 percent worldwide, is Shi'a. In North America, because of different immigration patterns, about 70 percent of Muslims are Sunni and 30 percent are Shi'a. Within the Shi'a tradition, there is a further split between the Ithna'ashari Shi'a and the Ismailis.

In addition, Islam contains a spectrum between liberals and conservatives. Just as there are moderate and radical

Christians and Jews, so there are moderate and radical Muslims. Unlike Judaism and Christianity, however, Islam has no official denominations within it. Although certain Muslims may identify themselves as moderate or liberal, there is no "Reform Islam" as there is Reform Judaism. Muslims who actively seek to implement Islamic law as a political reality, whether in the West or elsewhere, are referred to as Islamists [not to be confused with *Islamicists*, scholars of Islam].

Muslims also differ in the political systems that govern them. In Iran, Muslims live in a theocracy, where Islamic religious law is the law of the land. Others, such as those in Pakistan or Libya, live under a military dictatorship. Some, like Saudi Arabians, live under a monarchy. Others, such as Turks or Indians, live under secular democracies. In the West, Muslims live as minorities in plural, democratic societies.

2

Who are the Muslims?

Each morning as I drive to Loyola Marymount University, I pass the giant Anheuser-Busch Brewery in Van Nuys, California. The complex is a daily reminder of my working class origins. Born in Pakistan, I immigrated to Canada with my family when I was four. We lived in the Parkdale area of Toronto, an area as heavily populated by new Canadians as it is now. My father, Iqbal, worked first as an auto mechanic in Toronto, but soon found another job on an assembly line in neighbouring Oakville, building trucks for the Ford Motor Company. My mother, Feroza, also worked in factories, building parts for the automotive industry. After high school I spent summers at Ford with my father, earning a great deal of money and hating my job.

In many ways, we were a typical immigrant success story. Our parents worked hard at whatever jobs they could find so that their children could have a better life than they did. It was from them that I first learned to appreciate what Woody Guthrie called "the poetry of ordinary lives." At Ford, I learned about the poetry of the assembly line through the songs of Bob Seger. Later, as an academic, I was disappointed to learn that not many academics were concerned with the lives of ordinary people. I like to think that I have that concern, and I am unabashed in my love for professional wrestling and the Canadian television show *Trailer Park Boys*.

Our family was part of a large wave of immigrants to Canada in the 1970s. All of these new Canadians lived out their own individual poems. More than a decade earlier, however, a British convert to Islam had arrived in Toronto. Murray Hogben would eventually help me in my doctoral research through an account of his early experiences with Muslims in Toronto. His story symbolizes much of the story of Muslim immigrants in North America, but it also throws light on the larger question of who the world's Muslims really are. So I quote him at length.*

The poetry of a Muslim immigrant
by Murray Hogben[1]

When I arrived in Toronto in the summer of 1958, the Muslim community was still in its infancy. The first Muslims in the city must have been Arab peddlers from what is now Lebanon. These merchants had travelled all across North America since the mid-19th century and settled as scattered individuals or families based on their retail goods stores or even northern fur-trading posts. Some of these had congregated in Truro, Nova Scotia; Montreal, Quebec; the Ontario cities of Ottawa, Windsor, and London; and Edmonton, Alberta, where the first mosque in Canada was built in 1938.

The first non-Lebanese Muslims in Toronto at the turn of the century were from the still-extant Ottoman Empire, and included Albanians. Among the latter was Regep (Rajjab) Assim, who immigrated in 1912–13, apparently as a political refugee because of the failure of the Albanian independence movement in which he was involved.

*The excerpt has been edited considerably for length and flow.

Assim told me that he and his brothers were denied work in Toronto because they were Muslim and because they were associated with the Turks. Canadians abhorred the Turks for their treatment of Christian revolts in the latter days of the Turkish-dominated Ottoman Empire. During World War I the Turks were enemies of the Allies, as were the Ukrainians and East Europeans who belonged to the German and Austro-Hungarian Empires. At first, Assim and his brothers were self-employed, making candy. From there they went on to set up High Park Sweets on Bloor Street West. Eventually they became integrated into the community and its politics.

When I arrived in Toronto, the only existing Muslim association was the Albanian Muslim Society of Toronto, headed by Assim. The society hosted congregational meals on the major Muslim holidays [see Chapter Five] but had little else in the way of organization or facilities. Assim conducted funeral prayers and other services needed by his co-religionists. The group had also organized a very small Sunday school class that met in the basement of the home of Sami and Fetime Kerim.

Sami and Fetime were the first Muslims I met in Toronto. I went to their home to learn more about Islam, and while there encountered Pakistani and Lebanese Muslims. There were also some Bosnians from Yugoslavia who had come to Canada, along with Albanians, following the political strife of World War II and the communist takeover of Eastern Europe. These people all varied in their sense of religiosity, but many looked up to their imam, Regep Assim, who in turn looked after their interests. For many years, Assim would often fish out extra money from his pocket or write a cheque if we were short of money to pay our expenses.

Early in the 1960s, as the group became increasingly diverse, we dropped the Albanian moniker and renamed ourselves the Muslim Society of Toronto. Around that time, we had enough money to buy a former workshop at 3047 Dundas St. West, and established a shop-front "Islamic Centre." It had an upstairs apartment that we rented out, a finished basement, and a long main floor with a meeting room in front and a prayer room in the back. I remember painting some simple Indian or Islamic arch patterns on the walls. Hassan Karachi, a handsome Bosnian post-war arrival and owner of Niagara Protective Coatings, generously provided all the pale green and white paint, including for the basement floor.

Because of work schedules and the centre's distance from the homes of our members, we held our congregational prayers on Sundays rather than Fridays. I remember the first time I said prayers there, along with Assim, the society's secretary Badrul Hasan, and a few others. We prayed on one white sheet, dressed in our overcoats because of the cold.

Once we opened our doors, the number of Muslims who came for prayers slowly began to increase. Some older members had never learned how to pray, or had forgotten, so they would come to observe. We would hold our small formal meeting in rows of chairs in the front portion of the building, with 20 or 30 of us in attendance. We would listen to a *khutba* (sermon) by Assim or perhaps myself, and a reading from the Qur'an, followed by prayers in the back room. Afterwards, in the basement room, we would share coffee and something sweet.

We also had a small Sunday school for the children, and a small library. The building also hosted many social occasions. Our Eid dinners and other festivities often included the dancing of those Middle Eastern Dubke line dances popular with

Bosnians, Albanians, and some Arabs. Men and women mixed together at these events, and we all had a jolly time with no perceived impropriety.

By the late 1960s the number of Indo-Pakistani immigrants increased, disturbing the balance among the different cultural groups. This led to a series of disagreements over what was "Islamic" – including discussions of the Dubke dances. The president of those years was Dr. M.Q. Baig, an Indian professor of Islamic studies at the University of Toronto. I had originally encouraged Dr. Baig to come into the society because he had the kind of knowledge and understanding we lacked. He served the Society well for several years.

Unfortunately, however, differences between many of the newcomers and the original group escalated into an unseemly squabble. Those of us in the core group led by Baig managed to hold out while the more activist newcomers left to form the Islamic Foundation. While time has bridged the gap, the developing struggle between "moderate" and "fundamentalist" Islam was very heated and disturbing at the time, especially since we were still so few in number.

The Foundation bought a building on Rhodes Avenue in the east end of the city. The Society, in turn, sold the Dundas St. building and bought the more imposing Presbyterian church on Boustead Avenue, renaming it the Jami Masjid (mosque). We took out all the church pews and covered the floor with wall-to-wall carpeting, with strings laid down to mark the lines for prayers. To our relief, the few Presbyterians left in the changing district took away the one notably Christian stained-glass window. We also bought a section of the Glendale Memorial Gardens where a number of Muslims were buried, including, eventually, Regep Assim. (However, the exclusivity of the section was not sustained because not enough Muslims bought plots.)

We resumed Sunday prayers, but now some people came for Friday Jum'a prayers too. Our numbers increased dramatically with the late 1960s influx of groups whom the immigration quota system had previously excluded from Canada. The new building allowed for bigger festivities and a bigger Sunday school. Still, all this was not without cost to the original membership, or to moderate Islam. More fundamentalist Muslims flocked in, and Tablighi Jamaat [a proselytizing organization described below] groups camped in the prayer room and occupied its corners with their bedding. The multi-cultural balance of the earlier years seemed compromised.

Later, the Jami Masjid was sold to the Islamic Society of North America (ISNA). ISNA was the outgrowth of the earlier, more militant Muslim Students Association of North America, or MSA, also led by more recent immigrants. Eventually, the alternative to the ISNA became the fairly moderate Council of Muslim Communities of Canada (CMCC) formed in 1973. The CMCC gave a Canadian face to the rather American-dominated Federation of Islamic Associations of the United States and Canada. The CMCC held annual conferences, sponsored children's summer camps, and supported the Canadian Council of Muslim Women. Both the CMCC and the ISNA continue to be strong, and the differences that gave rise to their formation still exist.

The beginnings of Islam

Hogben gives us a wonderful vignette of the development and diversity of Muslim life in Toronto. To help set the context for an exploration of the broader Muslim scene in the world, however, we should survey briefly the origins of Islam. Where we begin, though, depends on whether or not we are Muslims. For non-Muslims, the story of Islam begins with the birth of the Prophet Muhammad in 570 C.E. in the Arabian city of Mecca. But for Muslims, the story begins much earlier, with the story of Adam, the first created human being.

Muslims do not see Islam as a new religion, introduced to the world after Judaism and Christianity. Instead, they see it as the primordial religion of God's creation. For Muslims, Muhammad was not the first prophet, nor the only one, but the last in a long line of prophets that God sent to help guide humanity. Muslims understand Muhammad to be the final prophet who brought God's revelation, the Qur'an, to humanity (see Chapter Four). When Muhammad died in the year 632 in the city of Medina, he was the head of a Muslim community that had spread across the Arabian Peninsula.

Within a century of Muhammad's death, Islam spread far outside the confines of Arabia. Muslims went west across North Africa, north into Europe (particularly Spain, France, Italy, and Sicily), and east to India and China. One of the most decisive battles in history was fought in 732, near the city of Tours, France (or Poitiers, as it is sometimes also known). Here, Charles Martel defeated the Muslim army, stopping the expansion of Islam into Northern Europe (see Chapter Six).

The spread of Islam is illustrated by a survey of the cities that became centres of power in the Muslim world. Religiously, Mecca is still the most important city for Muslims. It is here that Muslims believe that Abraham, along with his son Ishmael, built the first place of prayer to the one true God. Mecca is also where Muhammad was born and lived most of his life. In 622,

Muhammad moved north to Medina, where he lived until his death. His tomb in Medina remains a holy site for all Muslims.

Finally, for Shi'a Muslims the city of Kufa is another city with religious importance. Located in present-day Iraq, Kufa is where Muhammad's son-in-law and fourth successor, Ali, ruled as caliph (or for Shi'a Muslims, as the first Imam) in the mid-seventh century. After the period of the four caliphs (Muhammad's immediate successors) came the Umayyad Dynasty, which ruled from 661 to 750. The Umayyads were the first great builders in Islam. In 691 they erected the Dome of the Rock in Jerusalem, the third most important city for Muslims after Mecca and Medina, on the spot where Muslim tradition holds that Muhammad ascended to heaven. Umayyad power was concentrated in the Syrian city of Damascus, where the Great Mosque was built in 710.

The Umayyads were defeated by the Abbasid Dynasty, which ruled from 750 to 1258. The Abbasids, centred in Iraq, built Baghdad as their capital city in 762. Baghdad became one of the greatest centres in the intellectual history of the world. Many people who are not familiar with Islamic history know the literature of the *Thousand and One Nights* (sometimes translated as *The Arabian Nights*), whose setting is the time of the Abbasid ruler Harun al-Rashid.

Rivals struggled for power during these times, establishing their own kingdoms around other centres of power. An Islamic regime in Southern Spain, Al-Andalus, lasted seven hundred years following the conquest of Gibraltar in 711. Like Baghdad, Cordoba and Granada in Spain were also intellectual and cultural centres. Another rival to the Abbasids was the Fatimid Caliphate, which built the city of Cairo, Egypt, and established Al-Azhar University in 969.

Into the second millennium, the centres of power multiplied. In 1191, the Sultanate of Delhi was established. The Safavid Dynasty of Iran began in 1503. Islamic presence also took root in Central Asia, particularly in the cities of Bukhara, Samarqand, and Tashkent. Through trade, Islam was introduced to Southeast Asia, and with the partition of the Indian subcontinent into India and Pakistan in 1947, Indonesia became the most populous Muslim nation. Islam was also present in Africa, particularly in the kingdoms of Mali and Ghana.

The Abbasid Dynasty came to an end in 1258, when the Mongols sacked Baghdad. The next great dynasty to arise was the Ottoman Empire, which lasted from 1299 until the Republic of Turkey came into existence in 1923. The Ottomans captured Constantinople in 1453 and turned it into their capital, Istanbul. During this time, and even beyond the fall of the Ottoman Empire, European Christians knew the Ottomans as the Turks – the important enemy or "other" in Europeans' self-understanding.

A short survey of Muslim demographics in North America

Many North Americans are surprised to learn that Muslims have a long history on their continent. Historians estimate that 20 percent of the slaves who came from West Africa were Muslim. The connection between Islamic civilization and the Americas, however, begins even earlier. When Christopher Columbus set sail for what he believed would be India, he recognized that the people there might not speak his language, or the Castilian of his royal patrons. So he brought with him someone who could speak the language of the "other" civilization: Arabic. Luis de Torres was a *converso*, a Jew who was forced to convert to Christianity during the period in Spain known as the Reconquista, when the Roman Catholic Church purged Spain of its intertwined Islamic and Jewish heritage. Because of his heritage, Torres knew Arabic.[2]

As already noted in Murray Hogben's story, the first Muslim immigrants to North America other than slaves were from the Ottoman Empire in the late nineteenth century and the first half of the twentieth century. Many were itinerants who came to make money and then return to their countries of origin. Some, however, were farmers and settled permanently. Mosques sprung up in Cedar Rapids, Iowa, and Ross, North Dakota. In 1938, immigrants built the Al-Rashid Mosque outside of Edmonton, Alberta, thought to be the first mosque built in Canada.

In the last half-century, the Muslim population has increased dramatically through immigration, strong birth rates, and conversion. The first census in Canada, in 1871, counted 13 Muslims in Canada. A century later, there were an estimated 33,370 Muslims in Canada. By the time of the 1981 census, this number had almost tripled to 98,165. The figures from the 1991 census showed 253,260 Muslims in Canada, more than 2.5 times the number from 1981. The 2001 census listed 579,600 Muslims in Canada, increasing by 2.3 times over the previous decade. Islam was now the second-largest religious tradition in Canada – well behind Christianity, but ahead of Judaism.

The United States census does not ask the question of religious affiliation, so there is less certainty about the size of its Muslim population. I have seen estimates as low as two million people, and as high as ten million. My own research of America's immigration patterns, birth rates, and conversion rates – similar to those of Canada – leads me to conclude that both of these estimates are extreme. Since the population of the

United States is roughly ten times that of Canada, the figure should be about 5.4 million American Muslims. The figure is likely higher, however. It is possible that the United States attracts more immigrants because of greater opportunities in certain fields. (I am one, for example, who moved from Canada to the United States.) But the main reason is that a percentage of African Americans are Muslim; Canada has very few African Canadian Muslims. African American scholars estimate that there are at least one to 1.5 million African American Muslims. Add that to the 5.4 million projection, and the result is six to seven million American Muslims.

Diversity within Muslim communities

On the first day of my world religions courses, I tell my students something that I will repeat throughout the course: "If you are going to learn one thing in this course it is that there is no one way to be anything." Many of us are interested in the differences among religions, but sometimes the most important differences can be found within a religious tradition. There are no more than 15 million Jews in the world, for example, yet this small group contains tremendous diversity. One can point to doctrinal differences between Orthodox, Conservative, Reconstruction, and Reform Jews. Ethnically, Sephardic Jews live in Spain, the Middle East, and North Africa, while the Ashkenazi hail from Europe. Iranian and Ethiopian Jews are also distinct groups. Differences of religious observance divide ultra-Orthodox and secular Jews – for example, in the adherence to kosher dietary laws. Some Jews are interested in mystical traditions (such as Kabbalah or Hasidism) while others have no use for mystical experiences. Some Jews see religion deeply connected to their political lives, while others see religion as a private matter.

Often, people are aware of the differences within their own groups but assume other groups to be homogeneous. There is usually nothing malicious about this; it just emerges from simple ignorance. When I moved from Toronto to Los Angeles in 1997, for example, I was aware of the large Latino population. Naively, I assumed that all Spanish speakers in Los Angeles had some connection to Mexico. I soon realized that this was simply wrong. Yes, there were many from Mexico, but others had roots in Cuba, Spain, Texas, El Salvador, Honduras, Argentina, or Guatemala.

In a similar way, a wide diversity exists in the Muslim world. If we think of the diversity among 15 million Jews around the world, or among more than 300 million people of Christian heritage in North America, how much more diversity is found among the one billion Muslims around the world. A glance at the variety of origins among North American Muslims reveals the great ethnic diversity of the Muslim world: In Canada, the majority of Muslims are South Asian. In the United States, about 35 percent are South Asian, 33 percent Middle Eastern, and 25 percent are African American. There are also significant numbers of converts to Islam from diverse ethnic traditions. Some Muslims seek to make their society more Islamic by implementing Islamic religious law, while others seek to keep their Islam outside of the public and political spheres.

But in addition to these cultural and political differences, there are also significant religious variations among the world's Muslims. In broad strokes, here is just a brief survey of the main groups.

The Sunni-Shi'a split

The main division within Islam is between the Sunni and the Shi'a. To call this "only" a political split diminishes its significance. At bottom, it is a question of deeply held religious beliefs around the family of the Prophet Muhammad. The Shi'a understand themselves to be a people who are deeply devoted to the household of Muhammad, and it is from this devotion that the political differences spring.

As described in the next chapter, Muhammad died suddenly in the year 632. He had four daughters, but no sons that survived past infancy. Given the patriarchal nature of his society, the lack of a male heir would lead to problems of succession. Muhammad was believed to be God's last prophet, through whom God had revealed the final revelation, the Qur'an. The Muslim community could not, of course, replace him in that capacity. However, Muhammad was more than the final prophet. He was the religious head of the community, the leader of the congregational prayers, and the arbiter of religious disputes. He was also a political figure, since the Muslim tradition was dominant in much of Arabia at the time of his death.

The majority community claimed that Muhammad had left no successor. They came to be known as the Sunni, after the Arabic word for "tradition." They believed that they were following the tradition of Muhammad, and that it was up to the community to choose the best qualified leader from among them. The person they chose was Abu Bakr, one of the respected elders of the Muslim community. Today, about 80 percent of the Muslim world are Sunni. (This book is also written from a Sunni perspective.)

A minority community, however, held a different opinion. They were deeply devoted to the household of the Prophet, and particularly to Muhammad's cousin Ali, who was married to Muhammad's daughter Fatima. Through their marriage, Muhammad had grandsons, Hassan and Hussain, upon whom the Prophet doted when they were young. This community came to be known as the Shi'at Ali, or the "party of Ali," later known as the Shi'a. For them, Ali was the appropriate successor to Muhammad. They based this claim on the Qur'an, which speaks in lofty terms of the "people of the house" of Muhammad. Moreover, their own tradition says that Muhammad himself nominated Ali as his successor.

Groups within the Shi'a tradition

For the Shi'a, then, Ali was the first Imam. The word *imam* has multiple meanings. Literally, it refers to a prayer leader. When two or more Muslims pray together, one is designated as the imam, who stands in front and leads the prayer. Sunnis also use it as the title for someone who does this on a regular basis as the leader of a mosque. For Shi'a Muslims, however, the word also refers to the legitimate leader of the Muslim community after Muhammad. After Ali, this office was passed on to his son, Hassan, Muhammad's grandson. Among the Shi'a are different groups that acknowledge different lines of Imams (capitalized here to distinguish them as the supreme leaders, not local prayer leaders).

The Imami. The largest group is known as Imami or Twelver, who follow a line of twelve Imams after Muhammad. The group believes the twelfth Imam went into hiding in 941. For the Imami the last Imam is neither dead nor in heaven, but simply absent from the world. They believe he will return at the end of time to wage a final conflict between the forces of good and evil. In this way, we can think of the Imami Shi'a as a messianic movement, awaiting the return of the 12th Imam.

Meanwhile, in place of the hidden Imam are temporal authorities whom believers should follow as life models. The most learned of these are given the honorific title of *ayatollah* (sign from God). While following the ayatollahs (there are a number, serving various communities), believers wait for the return of the hidden Imam.

Imami Shi'a faith is dominant in Iran, Iraq, and Lebanon, but is present in many other countries as minority populations. Following the Iranian Revolution in 1979, many of those who left Iran were Shi'a, but they also included Iranian Jews, Baha'is, atheists, and others. The majority of them settled in the West, thereby increasing the Shi'a population. Today, for example, Los Angeles is thought to have the second-largest urban Iranian population outside of Tehran.

Ismailis. A smaller group of Shi'a are the Ismailis. They draw their name from Ismail, the seventh in a line of Imams that is different from that of the Imami. The Ismaili are unique in that they believe that the line of Imams continues till today. Their current Imam is His Highness, the Aga Khan, who currently resides in France. The Ismaili community numbers about 15 million in 28 countries around the world. Under the leadership of the Aga Khan, Ismailis have become perhaps the most integrated Muslim community in the West. Ismailis have places of worship known as *jamaatkhanas* (places of meeting), and do not worship in mosques. In colonial days, many Ismailis moved from the Indian subcontinent to East Africa to work with the British. In 1972, when the Ugandan dictator, Idi Amin, expelled Indians from Uganda, many Ismaili Muslims relocated to Canada and the United States.

Zaydis and Alawis. Two other groups of Shi'a are the Zaydis and Alawis. The Zaydis have a lineage of five Imams, the fifth being a grandson of Hussain named Zayd. The Zaydis are a strong minority presence in Yemen. Another group are the Alawis, who extend the devotion that other Shi'a groups apply to Ali. The Alawis are found in Turkey, Syria, and Lebanon, and number at least seven million.

Sunni Islam

As mentioned earlier, the Sunni community is the largest Muslim community, and does not have major religious factions within it. With the exception of Iran, Iraq, and Lebanon, Sunnis are the majority in any country with a Muslim population. The four countries with the largest Muslim population – Indonesia, Pakistan, India, and Bangladesh – all have a substantial Sunni majority. However, this is not to say that Sunnis are homogeneous. There are ethnic and cultural differences among them, such as the foods used to break the fast during Ramadan, or the architectural style of mosques.

Heterodox groups

In addition to Sunnis and Shi'as there are several smaller heterodox groups that other Muslims may dissociate from true Islam. Of course, the groups think of themselves as true Muslims and assume that other Muslims are the heterodox ones. I describe two such groups in some detail, since they are not well-known in North America, yet influential nonetheless.

Ahmadiyya. The Ahmadiyya community is very active in the promotion of their beliefs, and they publish a large number of pamphlets and booklets. The Ahmadis take their name from Mirza Ghulam Ahmad (1835–1908), who lived in what is now Pakistan. According to one of the pamphlets published by the community, in 1889 Ahmad "founded the Ahmadiyya Muslim Jama'at, under Divine guidance. Its main objective is to re-establish the original purity and beauty of Islam." In 1914, the community split into two factions, one based in the city of Qadian, India, and the other in Lahore, in what is now Pakistan. With the partition of India and the creation of Pakistan in 1947, the Qadian community moved to Rabwah, a new city in Pakistan.

The Ahmadiyya's acceptance of Mirza Ghulam Ahmad as the *Mahdi*, or "divinely guided one," led other Muslims in Pakistan and elsewhere to declare the Ahmadis to be non-Muslims in 1974 and again in 1984. Because of the resulting persecution, the head of the community, Mirza Tahir Ahmad, moved from Pakistan to London, England. As head of the community and grandson of Mirza Ghulam Ahmad, he is referred to as Khalifatul Masih IV (the fourth successor of the Messiah).

The Ahmadi community has a history of missionary activity outside of India and Pakistan. Following the establishment of the London Mission in 1914, Ahmadiyya missionaries began their work in North America, where they would not be persecuted and could proclaim their faith freely. The Lahore branch of the community is active in the United States, publishing material from its American headquarters in Columbus, Ohio. In Canada, the Ahmadiyya community began to grow in the 1970s, thanks to immigrant-friendly changes in Canadian immigration laws in 1967. In 1992 they opened the largest mosque in Canada, the Bait-ul-Islam (house of Islam) in Maple, Ontario.

Tablighis. The Tablighi Jamaat (community of informing) is also active in North America. The Jami Masjid mentioned in Hogben's account served as the first North American base of operations for the Tablighis in the late 1960s and early 1970s. In 1987 they established the Al Rashid Islamic Institute in Toronto to educate boys. Today they operate several other mosques across North America. The Tablighis make an organized effort to invite non-Muslims into Islam and to invite Muslims to accept their conservative interpretation of Islam. In some ways they are similar to some evangelical Christians who have conservative views of their traditions, see their interpretation as the only correct interpretation, and invite others to that interpretation.

Sufism: the mystical tradition

Like some Christians and Jews, some Muslims are attracted to mystical interpretations of their religion. Islam's mystical tradition is known as Sufism. This stream, described in detail in Chapter Eight, transcends Sunni and Shi'a sectarian differences in much the same way that Christian mysticism transcends Protestant, Catholic and Orthodox traditions, even though the mystics arise from those traditions. A number of Sufi groups are active in North America, representing the full spectrum of interpretations of Islam, from ultra-conservative to very liberal. Estimates in both Canada and the United States show that no more than one-quarter to one-third of North American Muslims attend mosque services. While many of these are secular Muslims who come from Muslim families but don't practice Islam and may not even believe in God, many of these non-attenders find their expressions of religiosity in groups that follow Sufism.

3

Muhammad: the beloved Prophet

In 2006, people around the world debated a Danish newspaper's publication[1] of a dozen cartoons about the Prophet Muhammad. The bitter controversy raised a number of questions, ranging from the role of images in Islam to violence in the contemporary Muslim world. The cartoons were discussed in forums as scholarly as the American Academy of Religion, and as popular as the animated television show *South Park*.

As a Western Muslim I had mixed responses. My Western roots taught me to value freedom of expression and the freedom of the press. Having spent time in certain parts of the Muslim world where the state controls the media, I much prefer the freedoms of North American society. While corporations control much of the media, a lively independent media is free to bring some balance and objectivity. My Muslim roots, however, teach me to value the life of the Prophet Muhammad. He is like a member of my family – a beloved and respected elder. I feel a strange need to protect him from unjust criticism in the same way that I would protect my parents, my siblings, my teachers, or my friends. Many Muslims will not even say his name without adding the formula "May God bless him and give him peace" or "Peace be upon him."

When I first saw the controversial cartoons, I thought of the novelist and literary critic, Salman Rushdie. Many people know Rushdie only as the author of *The Satanic Verses*, a novel that earned him a death sentence from Iran's Ayatollah Khomeini in 1989 and forced Rushdie into hiding until 1998. In the 1980s, however, Rushdie had also been involved in campaigns against racism in Britain. In an essay entitled "The New Empire Within Britain," he wrote about how Britain, once a powerful Empire, was now colonizing itself by creating ghettos for people of South Asian and African ancestry.

In his 1984 essay, "Outside the Whale," Rushdie wrote about the "Raj revival" that was taking place in Britain – a wave of nostalgia for the British colonial rule in India. Commenting on the television series *The Far Pavilions* and *The Jewel in the Crown*, he wrote:

> It would be easy to conclude that such material could not possibly be taken seriously by anyone, and that it is therefore unnecessary to get worked up about it... I would be happier about this, the quietist option... if I did not believe that it matters, it always matters, to name rubbish as rubbish; that to do otherwise is to legitimize it. I should also mind less, were it not for the fact that [it] is only the latest in a very long line of fake portraits inflicted by the West on the East... Stereotypes are easier to shrug off if yours is not the culture being stereotyped; or, at the very least, if your culture has the power to counterpunch against the stereotype.

Two decades later, the same thing would happen with the Danish cartoons. A number of non-Muslim cartoonists would create their own stereotypes of the Prophet Muhammad that would be deeply offensive to Muslims. The media discussions that ensued, usually quite simplistic in nature, revolved around freedom of expression. What was rarely discussed was that this was simply another in that "very long line of fake portraits." When Muslims became upset, they were termed fanatical and intolerant, even if they expressed their hurt through lawful and peaceful protests.

In many ways, the Rushdie affair was similar to the cartoon controversy. First, the initial protests were ignored. British Muslims objected to *The Satanic Verses* in October, 1988, through contact with the publishers and the government. This got them nowhere. On December 2, a small group burned the book in protest, but this also got no media attention. It wasn't until a group in Bradford burned the book on January 14, 1989, that the media began to pay attention, mostly because the group thought to invite them. The book burning led to a

Burning The Satanic Verses

The book-burning incident led to a torrent of denunciation. Muslims were called 'barbarians,' 'uncivilized,' 'fanatics,' and compared to the Nazis. Many a writer, some of impeccable liberal credentials, openly wondered how Britain could 'civilize' them and protect their innocent progeny against their parents' 'medieval fundamentalism.' Hardly anyone appreciated that the burning of *The Satanic Verses* was more an act of impatience than of intolerance, and that it bore no resemblance to the Nazi burning of libraries and persecution of intellectuals. No one cared to point out either that only a few months earlier, several Labour Members of Parliament had burnt a copy of the new immigration rules outside the House of Commons without raising so much as a murmur of protest.

– Bhikhu Parekh,
member of the House of Lords, London.

flurry of denunciations, and accusations of Nazi-like intolerance in the Muslim community.

Second, Muslim voices urged calm and an end to violence. In 2006, major Muslim groups in North America called on Muslims upset by the cartoons to remain peaceful, just as they had urged North American Muslims to remain calm during the Rushdie affair some 15 years earlier. The Canadian Islamic Congress (CIC), for example, called for a "calm period of healing" after the cartoons sparked worldwide protests. Unfortunately, these Muslim voices for peace were seldom heard in the mainstream media.

Third, in each case, some Muslim leaders around the world assumed roles as "defenders of Islam," inciting more hatred. In 2006 a Pakistani cleric, for example, reportedly offered a $25,000 reward for killing one of the cartoonists. However, this action was denounced by other Muslims. Dr. Mohamed Elmasry, the national president of the CIC commented, "What has been said and done by this irresponsible individual is totally against the teachings of the Qur'an, which condemns the taking of human lives... Only God is ultimate arbiter and judge of those who do wrong."

Let me be clear about my own views. While I disapprove of the cartoons, I defend the right of the press to publish them. I oppose any form of violent protest against the cartoons. I also reject the retaliatory acts of the Muslim media, such as publishing offensive cartoons about the Holocaust. Even so, I wonder what was to be gained in publishing the cartoons, especially since the same newspaper had earlier refused to print offensive cartoons about Jesus. Such double standards are part of the history of polemical images of Muhammad, which I discuss later in this chapter.

The Muhammad in the cartoons is not my beloved Prophet. In this chapter, I hope that non-Muslim readers can know something of the love that Muslims have for the Prophet. One of his attributes, which is so often forgotten in times of tension between Muslims and non-Muslims, is mercy. When Muhammad came into a position of political power after decades of persecution, his first act was to forgive those who had persecuted him. His heart of mercy is also illustrated by this ancient account of the Prophet: "A dying child was once brought to the Prophet Muhammad (peace be upon him). When, on seeing the child's last breaths, the Prophet began to shed tears, one of his companions asked why he was crying. He replied: 'It is mercy that God has put in the hearts of God's servants, and God is merciful only to those of God's servants who are merciful to others.'" I hope that in the midst of public debate between Muslims and non-Muslims, we all can be merciful to each other.

Prophets in Islam

Like Jews and Christians, Muslims have a prophetic history. God gives guidance to humanity by sending prophets who tell us how to live. For Muslims, Muhammad is not the first prophet, nor the only prophet, but the one who brings God's final revelation to humanity. The Qur'an mentions a number of other prophets by name, including the Old Testament figures of Adam, Noah, Abraham, Isaac, Jacob, Moses, and David. Three are from the New Testament: Jesus, John the Baptist, and Zechariah, the father of John. Of the biblical prophets, Moses is named most often in the Qur'an – more than 200 times. Jesus is mentioned more than 90 times. By contrast, Muhammad is only mentioned by name four times. Although Muhammad is the final prophet, Muslims treat all prophets named in the Qur'an with honour, and the devout will always utter the formula "May peace be upon him" when they mention any of them by name.

Muslims consider Adam, the first created human being, to be the first prophet. The Qur'an's story of Adam's creation is similar to that of the book of Genesis, where God creates Adam out of clay and breathes life into him. In the Qur'an, however, God makes Adam God's representative and tells him the names of all things. God then asks all creation to bow down before Adam. When Satan disobeys, God casts him out of heaven but allows him to tempt humanity until the Day of Judgment. From the beginning, therefore, Muslims believe that God has given us freedom of choice; we can choose to obey God and the prophets, or we can obey Satan. The first people that Satan tempts are Adam and Eve; in the Qur'an they are both responsible for disobeying God's command not to eat from the forbidden tree. For their disobedience, Adam and Eve are cast out of heaven, and sent to live on earth for a time.

After Adam, God continues to send prophets to the world. Muslims see this provision as one of the many signs of God's mercy. Some prophets are given a text to pass along to humanity. The Qur'an mentions a lost text given to Abraham; the Psalms to David; the Torah to Moses; the Gospel to Jesus (but different from the New Testament); and finally, the Qur'an to Muhammad. (See Chapter Four for a discussion of these scriptures.)

For Jews, Christians, and Muslims alike, Abraham is the great patriarch, the first monotheist. In the Muslim tradition, Abraham comes to Mecca with his son Ishmael and there builds the first place of prayer to the one true God. This place, known as the Ka'ba, is the focus of the pilgrimage to Mecca (see Chapter Five). The story of Moses is also crucial to Muslims, and he is mentioned by name in the Qur'an more times than any other prophet. For Muslims, the story of the Exodus from Egypt is the archetypal story of the struggle against oppression. Pharaoh represents the reluctance of the world to listen to God's messengers. Moses represents the word of God, which ultimately triumphs in the release of the people of Israel from their slavery.

Many Christians are surprised to learn that Jesus is also an important prophet for Muslims. The Qur'an confirms that Jesus was born of Mary, a virgin. In fact, Mary, the virgin mother of Jesus, is named more often in the Qur'an (34 times) than she is in the New Testament (19 times). The 19th chapter of the Qur'an is entitled "The Chapter of Mary" and tells of the Annunciation in similar language to that used in Luke's gospel. For Muslims, however, the virgin birth, while making Jesus extraordinary, does not make him divine. If any prophet had a claim to divinity, it would be Adam, who was born without a male or female parent. (See Chapter Nine for more on Muslim and Christian understandings of Jesus.)

Muhammad's birth and early life

Muhammad was born in 570 CE in the Arabian city of Mecca, a centre of polytheistic worship. Muslims believe that between the time when Abraham and Ishmael built the Ka'ba and the time when Muhammad appeared, the Ka'ba had been turned into a shrine for the worship of many pagan gods and goddesses. At the time of Muhammad's birth, Judaism and Christianity were known, but there were no substantial communities of Jews or Christians in Mecca. A few people in the city, however, practiced a native Arabian form of monotheism.

Muhammad's early life was not happy. His father Abdallah, a caravan trader, died before Muhammad was born. In a tribal society where one's place was based on the father's identity, to be born without a father was a tremendous handicap. Muhammad was raised by his mother, Aminah, but she too died when Muhammad was six. Muhammad's grandfather, 'Abd al-Muttalib, raised Muhammad for the next two years until he also died. Clearly, Muhammad experienced a lot of sorrow in his young life. It is no surprise that as an adult, Muhammad would show a deep concern for the protection of orphan children.

After age eight, Muhammad was raised by an uncle, Abu Talib, who was also involved in the caravan trades. By working in his uncle's business, Muhammad travelled across Arabia. Muslim tradition tells how, on one such journey, he met a Christian monk who recognized him as a prophet of God. This marked the first connections between Islam and Christianity. It was also through his work as a trader that Muhammad met his wife, Khadija bint Khuwaylid. Khadija was a wealthy widow who was 15 years older than Muhammad. She knew of Muhammad's reputation for honesty and hired him to work for her. This business alliance turned into a relationship of love.

As we will see in more detail in Chapter Seven, the relationship was remarkable in many respects, and contradicts many stereotypes of patriarchy among Muslims. First, Khadija was older than Muhammad, and she had been married before. Second, Khadija was the wealthy one, and Muhammad was economically dependent on her. Third, she was the one who proposed marriage to him. Fourth, they remained in a monogamous marriage until her death. Muhammad and Khadija had four daughters, Zaynab, Ruqayyah, Umm Kulthum, and Fatima, as well as two sons who died in infancy. Muhammad,

Khadija, and their family prospered as Muhammad became a successful businessman and a pillar of his community. However, at the age of 40, something happened that would change Muhammad's life, and the world, forever.

The first revelations to Muhammad

Muslims believe that Muhammad did not practice the polytheism of his people, but that he was a monotheist. Often, like many of us who like to escape the city for a retreat in nature, he would pray and meditate in the hills surrounding Mecca. One night, in the year 610 CE, as he was meditating in a cave, the Angel Gabriel appeared to him in a vision. Gabriel (whom Jews and Christians also respect as a conveyor of divine revelation) commanded him to recite. Muhammad replied that he could not recite; he did not know what to recite. A second time, Gabriel commanded Muhammad to recite, and he received the same response. The third time Gabriel commanded Muhammad to recite, Gabriel wrapped Muhammad in his embrace and told him the words to recite. Eventually these words became the first five verses of the ninety-sixth chapter of the Qur'an:

> In the name of God the Compassionate the Caring
> Recite in the name of your Lord who created –
> From an embryo created the human
> Recite your Lord is all-giving
> Who taught by the pen
> Taught the human what he did not know before.[2]

When Muhammad had finished reciting the angel's words, Gabriel released him from his embrace. After Muhammad left the cave, he saw Gabriel in his true angelic form, large enough to fill the horizon.

Whether one believes this incident is factual depends on whether one is a Muslim. However, anyone can believe what happened next: Muhammad thought that he was going mad. Still shaking from the encounter, Muhammad returned home and told Khadija. Muslim tradition tells us that she did not think that he was mad or hallucinating; she believed Muhammad's report of what had just occurred. Moreover, she was the first to believe that Muhammad was the Messenger of God – the title that would remain with him from that point on. No longer would he be a businessman; he was God's messenger. The revelations that Gabriel gave to Muhammad that night would form the beginnings of the Qur'an, which means "the recitation."

Muhammad's public preaching

At first, Muhammad received no instructions to publicly proclaim the messages God had given him, so he preached only to his household. Later, however, he was commanded to preach the revelations to the people of Mecca. Not surprisingly, his message of monotheism did not go over well, given the polytheism of his society. Many Meccans earned their living from the pilgrimage trade, where people from the various tribes would come to the Ka'ba to pay homage to their deities. Not only was Muhammad's message of monotheism offensive to the Meccans; it was also potentially very bad for business.

Given Muhammad's prominence in Meccan society, however, his message was initially tolerated. But his community soon began to grow. For those at the bottom of the economically stratified society, conversion to the new religion could offer an equality not present in their ordinary lives. While many converts were from the lower classes, some were also from wealthy classes. Eventually, as Muhammad's community began to grow, it became a threat to the Meccans. Persecution increased toward new converts, especially those without the economic status that Muhammad had. Muhammad himself was under the protection of his uncle, Abu Talib, who was a prominent citizen of Mecca.

As opposition increased, Muhammad came up with a novel solution. He sent a number of his most vulnerable followers across the Red Sea to Abyssinia (modern day Ethiopia) – the first emigration of Muslims. This decision was remarkable and important because Abyssinia was a Christian country, ruled by a Christian king. Muhammad knew this, and assumed that the Christian ruler would protect the Muslim refugees because of the similarities between the two religions. This is indeed what happened, and the arrangement marks the first instance of Muslim-Christian dialogue. For this, Muslims have always owed a debt of thanks to Christians.

The "Year of Sadness" – Khadija and Abu Talib

Nine years after the first revelations, in 619, Muhammad experienced what Arabic sources call the "Year of Sadness" because it contained two deaths that deeply affected Muhammad. The first was the passing of his beloved Khadija. Although few scholarly sources discuss the impact of her death on Muhammad, we can imagine that it was great. She and Muhammad had been married for almost 25 years, almost exactly half of Muhammad's life. They had a loving family, with four daughters. They knew the grief of losing two other children in infancy. Moreover, Khadija was the first to believe in Muhammad as the Messenger of God.

After the death of Khadija, Abu Talib also died. Although Abu Talib was Muhammad's uncle, he was really the only father figure Muhammad knew. With Abu Talib dead, another uncle,

Abu Lahab, now became the head of Muhammad's family. While Abu Talib had protected Muhammad from persecution, Abu Lahab had no such love for his nephew. As a result, the persecution of the early Muslim community now extended to Muhammad himself.

The "Night Journey" and the "Ascension"

After the Year of Sadness came two related events that Muslims see as proof that God had not abandoned the Prophet: Muhammad's night journey to Jerusalem, and his ascension from Jerusalem to heaven. Muslim tradition holds that in 621 God took Muhammad from his home in Mecca to what the Qur'an refers to as "the farthest mosque," Jerusalem. Muslims debate whether this was a physical journey or a mystical experience, but they agree that his consciousness was transported to Jerusalem. The tradition is rich with images of this journey, including that of the magical winged horse that transported Muhammad. Some sixty years after Muhammad's death, the Muslim community would build the Al-Aqsa (farthest) Mosque on the site they believed Muhammad had visited.

From Jerusalem, Muslims believe, Muhammad ascended to heaven, into the very presence of God. On his journey through the "seven heavens" he encountered prophets from the past – a story that Miguel Asin claims was the basis for Dante's classic, *The Divine Comedy*.[3] The Dome of the Rock in Jerusalem was built over the spot where it is believed he ascended, and some Muslims claim to see the footprint of Muhammad in the rock. For Jews, the rock is the exposed surface of Mount Moriah, where Abraham offered up Isaac for sacrifice, and where Solomon later built the temple. The base of this temple survives as the western or "wailing" wall as it is popularly known. For

Muslims, this area is known as the Haram al-Sharif (the noble sanctuary), and is the third holiest place in Islam after the Ka'ba in Mecca and the Prophet's grave in Medina.

The hijrah and the first Islamic community

As persecution increased in Mecca, Muhammad realized he needed a new home. Help came in the form of an overture from the people of Yathrib, some 250 miles north of Mecca. Yathrib was an oasis city, with two large feuding Arab tribes and a number of smaller Jewish tribes. Muhammad, known for his honesty, was invited to arbitrate the dispute between the two Arab tribes. Once Muhammad moved to the city of Yathrib, it was renamed Medina al-Nabi (city of the Prophet), later shortened to Medina.

The move, which took place in 622, was known in Arabic as the *hijrah* (emigration). In Medina, a number of Muslim converts helped resettle the Muslim community from Mecca. Muhammad built a home that included a mosque where Muslims could worship openly. The ability of Muslims to exist now as a community free from persecution was so important to the Muslim community that the *hijrah* – not Muhammad's birth or the first revelation – became the beginning year in the Muslim calendar.

In some ways, the story of the *hijrah* mirrors the history of Christianity, albeit on a very compressed time scale. For the first three centuries of its existence, Christianity was a persecuted movement; it only became a protected movement in the fourth century when the Armenian kingdom and later the Roman Empire adopted Christianity as a state religion. In Islam, this shift happened 12 years after the first revelations to Muhammad. However, for the Muslim community, the intertwining of the political and the religious began on a more local level and grew from there. Muhammad established the covenant of Medina, stipulating that all were part of one Muslim community but giving religious freedom to the Jewish tribes (providing they did not threaten this Muslim state).

At first, the Meccans were relieved at Muhammad's departure. Now they did not have to deal with the embarrassment of one of their leading citizens denouncing their polytheism, as well as their economic livelihood, which depended on polytheism. However, in a short time, free from persecution, the Muslim community began to grow in Medina. This, together with lingering hostilities from the past, helped to fuel a series of battles between the Meccan polytheists and the Medinan Muslims.

The battles were essentially related to the economic survival of the Muslims who had migrated. When the Muslims abandoned their homes in Mecca, they left behind most of their property. Moreover, since they had been traders, they were unaccustomed to the agricultural life of Medina. The Battle of Badr in 624 emerged out of a Muslim raid on a Meccan caravan that contained goods that belonged to the Muslims. The Meccans waged the Battle of Uhud in 625 to avenge their loss in the first battle. Finally, the Meccans initiated the Battle of the Trench in 627, seeking to destroy the Muslims who had been weakened by their loss in the second battle. During this time, more and more people converted to Islam, strengthening the position of Muhammad and the Muslim community in Medina.

The return to Mecca and the death of Muhammad

In 630, eight years after he had to leave Mecca, Muhammad returned in triumph. Rather than waging all-out war, he decreed that he would only fight people who fought against him, and would not attack those who sought sanctuary. As a result, few people were killed in the Muslim conquest of Mecca. There, Muhammad showed the mercy that made him beloved among Muslims. He gathered together those who had persecuted him and driven him from his home. By tribal custom, he had the right to massacre them, but instead, he quoted the story from the Qur'an about Joseph and his brothers (which is similar to the Genesis story): "This day there shall be no upbraiding of you nor reproach. God forgives you, and God is the Most Merciful of those who show mercy" (Qur'an 12:92). With that, he gave everyone a general amnesty, which caused even more people to convert to Islam.

Muhammad cleansed the Ka'ba of the idols that it contained, rededicating it to the worship of the one true God. Then he returned to his home in Medina. In 632, Muhammad led a final pilgrimage to Mecca. The sermon he preached to his community at that occasion proved to be his farewell sermon; he fell ill later that year and died a few days later. He was buried where he died, in his home in Medina.

Muhammad in Muslim piety and memory

Muslims have a tremendous respect for the life of the Prophet Muhammad. Many Muslims around the world celebrate the birthday of the Prophet in a holiday known as the Mawlid. Those who are pious will not repeat his name without adding a formula of praise: "May God bless him and give him peace." This blessing follows an injunction in the Qur'an that says, "God and God's angels bless the Prophet. Oh you who believe, invoke God's peace and blessing upon him" (Qur'an 33:56). At the conclusion of the daily prayers (see Chapter Five), Muslims ask God to "send blessings on Muhammad and the family of Muhammad, just as you [God] sent blessings on Abraham and the family of Abraham." The high regard Muslims show for Muhammad is also evident in their faith statement, which consists of one sentence, "I bear witness that there is no god but God, and I bear witness that Muhammad is the Messenger of God."

Muhammad is seen as the model for Sufis, the mystics of Islam (see Chapter Eight). Sufis seek direct experience of the Divine, just as Muhammad did when he received the revelations and when he ascended into the presence of God. Sufis and non-Sufis alike sing many devotional songs to the Prophet Muhammad. One of my favourites, by Shaykh Muhammad ibn al-Habib of Morocco, ends with the lines:

Our gifts are from a Prophet [Muhammad] who is the master of the creations of God.
May the purest of blessings be upon him, in number great as the knowledge of God,
And on his family and companions, and everyone who calls to God.

Muslims do not consider Muhammad to be divine, however. This is why, in an earlier era, Muslims objected to being called "Mohammedans," implying that they worshipped him. Muhammad was a human of ordinary birth. This makes him different from Adam, who was created out of clay, not born of parents. It also makes him different from Jesus who, Muslims believe, was born of the Virgin Mary without a male parent. Even if Muhammad had had such beginnings, it would not have changed the central belief of Muslims: God is the only divine being.

When Muhammad died, his companion Abu Bakr is reported to have said to the crowd gathered at his door, "Oh you who worship Muhammad, know that Muhammad is dead. But you who worship God, know that God is alive and never dies." Abu Bakr then recited the following verse: "Muhammad is no more than a messenger; other messengers have passed away before him. Will it be that if he dies you will turn back upon your heels? Whoever turns back upon their heels will do no harm to God, and God will reward those who are thankful" (Qur'an 3:144).

Muslims are to pattern their life after Muhammad. The popular phrase among some Christians, "What would Jesus do?" resonates deeply with Muslims, who constantly seek to emulate what Muhammad would do. Muhammad's example is remembered in a body of literature known as the hadith (narratives). The hadith are the stories of what Muhammad said and did and resemble the honoured collections of sayings and stories about other historical religious figures, including the Buddha, Confucius, and Jesus.

Images of Muhammad – polemical and otherwise

Contrary to popular misconceptions, the reverence given to Muhammad has sometimes taken the form of images and pictures of Muhammad. This is particularly true in the Shi'a tradition, where to this day in Iran one can buy postcards with images of the Prophet or of his son-in-law, Ali. In both Sunni and Shi'a forms of Islam, one sees a rich tradition of paintings of Muhammad's night journey to Jerusalem and his ascension to heaven. In some of them, Muhammad's face is obscured by fire or a veil, while in others it is visible. In Muslim homes, one often sees a written description of the Prophet's features, done in elaborate calligraphy and displayed with great pride.

Unfortunately, non-Muslims have sometimes created negative images of Muhammad. The Danish cartoon controversy of 2006 is not new in the history of Christian-Muslim polemic. Dante, in his *Divine Comedy*, places both Muhammad and Ali in the ninth circle of hell, where they are tortured as "sowers of scandal and schism." This is doubly tragic when, as indicated earlier, Dante's work itself may have been based on the narrative of Muhammad's ascent to heaven. Dante wrote his work in the Middle Ages, when Islam was understood to be a Christian heresy and Muhammad as a renegade cardinal who started his own religion after a falling out with the Catholic Church. Such misinformation and hurt continues today. After 9-11, for example, one prominent Christian minister referred to the Prophet as a "terrorist" and another described him as "a demon-possessed pedophile."

Thankfully, these are not the only portrayals by Western non-Muslims. The writers Thomas Carlyle, George Bernard Shaw, and James Michener, have all portrayed Muhammad positively. A number of Christian ministers have reached out to Muslims and borne witness to their own faith without needing to attack Muhammad. Among them, close to my home, are Rev. Robert Schuller and his son Robert Jr., whose ministry at the Crystal Cathedral is broadcast as the *Hour of Power*. Some journalists have also recognized the positive influence of Muhammad. Michael Hart, in his book *The 100: A Ranking of the Most Influential Persons in History* put Muhammad at the top of his list. "[This choice] may surprise some readers and may be questioned by others," he wrote, "but [Muhammad] was the only man in history who was supremely successful on both the religious and secular level."

The root of the cartoon controversy was not that Muhammad was depicted in pictures, because Muhammad has been depicted artistically by Muslims. The problem is that he has been depicted as a terrorist, a debauched man possessed by the devil. This, clearly, is an image that causes Muslims to take great offence – just as many Christians raised an outcry at the release of Monty Python's *Life of Brian* and *The Last Temptation of Christ*. The life of Muhammad is just as important to Muslims as the life of Jesus is to Christians; it should therefore be told in a respectful, if not reverential, way. The issue is not simply freedom of expression, as it is often made out to be. It is about who has the power to create stereotypes, and how those stereotypes affect the way we treat people.

4

The Qur'an:
the Ultimate Revelation

On May 9, 2005, *Newsweek* published a story that claimed the Qur'an had been desecrated numerous times at the United States military prison at Guantanamo Bay, Cuba. This report set off protests around the Muslim world, some of them violent. Some 17 people were killed in Afghanistan. The following week, *Newsweek* apologized for its story, indicating it had no proof that the allegations came from a military report as originally claimed. But less than three weeks later, a report by the base commander, Brigadier General Jay Hood, did confirm five cases of the Qur'an's desecration after all. It had been splashed with urine, kicked, stepped on, damaged by water, and had an obscenity written inside the front cover.

Many non-Muslims could not see why Muslims would be so concerned about the way a book was handled. A comparison with the Christian view of "the Word," however, might help us understand. Christians, especially Protestants, have a high regard for their scriptures, just as Muslims do, and often refer to the Bible as the Word of God. For Christians the Word of God is also a term that applies to Jesus. The opening words of John's gospel beautifully describe Jesus in this way: "In the beginning was the Word, and the Word was with God, and the Word was God... And the Word was made flesh, and dwelt among us." A central article of Christian faith is that Jesus is God who comes to earth in the flesh, the Word Incarnate. Similarly, for Muslims, the Qur'an is the very Word of God, come to earth not in the form of a human, but in the form of a book, the Word "Inlibrate" if you will. Keep these analogies in mind throughout this chapter; the Qur'an is to Muslims what both the Bible and Jesus are to Christians.

Nature of the Qur'an in its present form

The word *Qur'an* translates as "the recitation." (*Koran* is a less accurate but acceptable transliteration of the Arabic word.) For Muslims, the only thing that can be called the Qur'an is the Arabic original, which they believe was revealed to Muhammad from 610 to 632 CE. For Muslims, God authored the Qur'an and Muhammad was simply the channel of revelation. It makes perfect sense, therefore, that the revelation would be sent down in the language spoken by Muhammad and those who first heard God's message.

Very quickly, however, Islam spread to places where Arabic was not the dominant language. Over the centuries, Muslims have translated the Qur'an into many languages. Indeed, several English translations have been published in the past few years. A look at the English titles, however, indicates that the translations do not completely capture the original Qur'an. The titles include *The Koran Interpreted, The Meaning of the Glorious Qur'an,* and *Approaching the Qur'an.* For Muslims, a translation of the Qur'an is the human product of a human translator, so it cannot be treated as being of divine authorship.

Even though 80 percent of Muslims do not speak Arabic as their primary language, it is only the Arabic text that is used liturgically. Muslims may read translations of the Qur'an in whatever language they understand, but for religious purposes such as the daily prayers, they will all recite the Arabic verses. This is similar to the use of Latin in Roman Catholic churches before the reforms of the Second Vatican Council. To be sure, many Muslims, like many pre-Vatican II Catholics, may not fully understand what they are saying in worship. Yet there is also something to be said for Muslims around the world reading the same text in the same language, especially if they believe that text to be the very Word of God.

In my own life, I have come across a delightful parallel. As mentioned previously, my late wife Shannon's family was Mennonite on her father's side. I remember one Christmas in Altona, Manitoba, where we started a discussion about something in the Bible. Before the conversation went very far, Grandma Hamm went to get a copy of what for her was the original, authoritative text: Luther's German translation.

In size, the Qur'an is roughly 80 per cent as long as the New Testament. It consists of 114 chapters, or *surahs* (enclosures) as they are known in Arabic. Muslims refer to the chapters by their chapter titles rather than the chapter numbers. The first chapter, for example, is entitled "The Opening," the 12th is "Joseph," and the 19th is "Mary." The chapters, in turn, are radically unequal in length. The second chapter is roughly the same length as the last 30 chapters combined. The smallest chapter is three verses long, while the longest chapter contains 286 verses. In Arabic, each verse is known as an *ayah* (sign) indicating that each verse is to be regarded as being of divine origin.

The Qur'an is not arranged chronologically, with the first chapter being the first one revealed and the 114th being the last. Instead, it is roughly arranged from longest to shortest, although the first chapter has only seven verses. While this arrangement may seem curious, it was a common way to order texts in the ancient world. One thinks, for example, of the apostle Paul's letters in the New Testament, with the longest letter of Romans placed at the beginning and the shortest letter of Philemon placed at the end of the Pauline section. To help facilitate a month's reading of the Qur'an, the book is further divided into 30 roughly equal parts that transcend chapter divisions. During Ramadan, Muslims will often read one part each night, thus completely reciting the text during the month.

Every chapter of the Qur'an except for the ninth begins with an invocation in Arabic known as the *basmalah*. This is usually translated as "In the name of God, the Merciful, the Compassionate." The Arabic text uses two words which are almost identical, *rahman* and *raheem*, to speak of the mercy and compassion that God has for all creation. These attributes are much more often in the Qur'an than the wrath of God. Interestingly, the root for both words is *rahm* (womb). What could be more merciful than a mother's womb, which gives shelter to her child?

Arabic, like every language, has its own conventions for poetry and prose – and the Qur'an is neither. There is a great deal of rhyme in the Qur'an, however – sometimes in the form of terminal rhymes, and other times in the form of rhyming phrases repeated throughout the text. In themselves these poetical aspects do not mark the Qur'an as poetry, but they increase its ease of memorization. (We can all remember the words to our favourite songs and poems more easily than we can remember our favourite prose pieces.) All Muslims memorize certain passages from the Qur'an, including the opening chapter, which is used in the daily prayers. Some Muslims commit the entire text to memory.

How the Qur'an came to us

In the last chapter, we discussed the beginnings of the revelation, when the angel Gabriel first appeared to the Prophet Muhammad in the cave near Mecca. Muslims believe that between that encounter in 610 and Muhammad's death in 632, he continued to receive divine revelations through Gabriel. While the Qur'an is not arranged chronologically, Muslims have a body of literature that tells when and under what circumstances certain verses were revealed. This information is sometimes found in commentaries on the Qur'an. Many Muslims will know some of the circumstances, but only those trained in the religious texts and sciences will know all of them.

In printed copies of the Qur'an, each chapter carries the designation "Meccan" or "Medinan," indicating when and where most of the chapter was revealed. The Meccan revelations occurred between 610 and 622, when Muhammad lived in Mecca. The Medinan revelations occurred after the emigration to Medina in 622. There are slight differences of opinion among Muslim scholars as to which chapters were revealed where. Between 86 and 90 chapters are classified as Meccan, while 24 to 28 chapters are classified as Medinan. The Meccan chapters are usually much shorter than the Medinan chapters, although one of the shortest chapters in the Qur'an, Chapter 110 ("The Help"), is Medinan.

Generally, the language of the Meccan chapters is the language of imperatives and exhortations. In fact, the first word to be revealed is the command, "Recite." Other imperatives are "glorify," "say," "warn," and "arise." The Meccan verses tend to be short, and they tell people that they should worship God. The later Medinan verses explain in detail how to worship. This is not surprising, in light of the fact that the verses were given at a time when Muslims could finally live and worship freely in community.

My favourite chapter is "The Morning" (Chapter 93), a Meccan chapter. It illustrates both the imperative tone of the Qur'an and the theme of God's compassion:

> In the name of God, the Merciful the Compassionate.
> By the morning,
> By the night when it is still,
> Your Lord has not forsaken you, nor is your Lord displeased,
> And the hereafter will be better for you than the present,
> And your Lord will give to you so you will be content.
> Did your Lord not find you an orphan and shelter you?
> And find you erring, and guide you?
> And find you needy, and enrich you?
> So do not treat the orphan harshly.
> Nor drive away the petitioner.
> And proclaim the bounty of your Lord.

The unconnected letters

First-time readers of the Qur'an are often surprised to discover that 29 of the chapters begin with letters, not words. These are known as the abbreviated or unconnected letters. Three chapters begin with a single letter, while others begin with a combination of up to five letters. In Chapters 20, 36, 38 and 50, these letters or combination of letters are used as the names of the chapters. When reciting these chapters, one recites the letters by themselves. Muslims have traditionally debated what these letters mean, and why they are in the text of the Qur'an. The standard understanding is that the true meaning of the letters is hidden, known only to God. Sometimes mystical meanings are associated with these letters, in much the same way that Hebrew letters carry hidden meanings in Jewish mysticism. Other times, it is explained that the letters are abbreviations for words. In Chapter 36, for example, the letters *ya* and *seen* could stand for the invocation "O human being."

The writing of the Qur'an

The Qur'an existed first as an oral tradition. Muhammad received the revelation and recited it to those who would listen. Muhammad did not simply remember the Qur'an; it was in some way imprinted upon his heart and tongue. As God's special messenger, he became the living receptacle of the Qur'an. Then, when he recited the text, others remembered it. Paper was known at this time in Arabia, but it was a scarce commodity. Even so, people who were literate wrote the verses as they heard them – on palm leaves, flat stones, and the shoulder bones of animals.

With the death of Muhammad and others who had memorized the Qur'an, it was necessary to put together an authoritative written text. Muhammad's first successor, Abu Bakr, commissioned Zayd ibn Thabit to consult with other memorizers of the Qur'an and compile the first complete copy of the Qur'an. Abu Bakr then entrusted the manuscript to Hafsah, one of the wives of the Prophet. (This point is important for those who think that Muslims place a low value on women. I do not know of a comparable early example in Judaism or Christianity, where a copy of the Torah or the Bible was given to a woman for safekeeping.)

At the bidding of Muhammad's third successor, Uthman (644–656), Zayd and three others made copies of the original manuscript that was entrusted to Hafsah. These were distributed to places where the Muslim tradition had spread. There is no consensus on how many copies were made and what happened to these manuscripts, but at least two of them are reputed to have survived to this day – one in a mosque in Tashkent, Uzbekistan, and the other at the Topkapi Museum in Istanbul, Turkey. Muslims believe that these and all subsequent copies of the Qur'an are identical to what was first revealed to the Prophet Muhammad.

There is a small group of non-Muslims who seek to discredit the Muslim view of the compilation of the Qur'an. Some of these are Jewish or Christian polemicists who hold to the divine authority of their own scriptures, but cannot accept the Muslim understanding that the Qur'an is the very Word of God. Some of these claim that the Qur'an was not written until several hundred years after Muhammad, and then only in response to Jews and Christians who had their own scriptures. These views that the Qur'an was compiled hundreds of years later are minority views, unsupported by ordinary Muslims or by the vast majority of Qur'an scholars, Muslim and non-Muslim alike.

This raises the question of historical-critical approaches to the scripture of a religion. For some time in Judaism and Christianity, scholars have applied these approaches to the study of the Bible, but usually with some skepticism from traditional believers. Most notably, in the 19th century Julius Wellhausen proposed a hypothesis that claimed Moses was not the author or scribe of the first five books of the Hebrew Bible, but that these books represented four separate sources that were later edited together. Many Jews and Christians accept this hypothesis, but some conservative believers reject it completely. Some Christians similarly have no interest in the claim of biblical scholarship that a now-hidden document known as "Q" was used in the composition of the Gospels of Matthew and Luke. They will claim, for example, that Matthew was composed by a person named Matthew, and that every word of the narrative is to be taken literally. Other Christians see no problems in reconciling historical-critical scholarship with their own faith, and will distinguish between "the Jesus of history and the Christ of faith."

Muslims, by contrast, are relatively new to the application of historical-critical scholarship on the Qur'an. In the past, this kind of scholarship was done not by Muslims but by Jewish and Christian scholars who wanted to discredit the authority of the Qur'an. Not surprisingly, most Muslims think that any kind of historical-critical scholarship is an attempt to undermine the Qur'an and its sacredness to Muslim life. However, Muslim scholars such as Mohammed Arkoun, Amina Wadud, and Farid Esack are among those trying to apply historical-critical scholarship to the Qur'an in much the same way that biblical scholars have done. This century may see some interesting developments in the ways in which Muslims will read and understand the Qur'an.

Other revelations

Just as Muhammad is considered the final prophet for Muslims, the Qur'an is the final revelation. Just as God had sent prophets before Muhammad, Muslims also believe that God had sent down previous revelations before the Qur'an. Of the prophets mentioned in the Qur'an, five conveyed divine messages that took written form: Abraham who was given a text that is now lost; Moses who was given the Torah; David who was given the Psalms; Jesus who was given the Gospel; and Muhammad who was given the Qur'an.

Christians are particularly interested in the Muslim view of the Gospel, which the Qur'an refers to as *injeel*, reminiscent of the Greek word *evangelion*. Muslims distinguish between the four Gospels of the New Testament and what they believe was revealed to Jesus. Muslims think that Jesus was given a particular text, but that this text was not preserved in its original form but later modified into the four Gospels of the New Testament. For Muslims, only the Qur'an is considered to be preserved in the original form in which it was first revealed. As a result, only the Qur'an is considered to be authentic scripture.

The fact that Muslims consider the Hebrew Bible and the Gospels to be different from what was actually revealed to Moses and Jesus does not mean they fault these prophets. They simply believe that over time, these originally pure messages were corrupted and mis-remembered by subsequent generations. That is why, they believe, God sent later messages to correct what had been misunderstood. Naturally, this is offensive to Jews and Christians, who do not think of their scriptures as inadequate for faith. However, this seems to be the nature of religious traditions that claim to supersede others.

As Christians believe that the New Testament confirms, adds to, and reinterprets the Hebrew Bible, so Muslims think that the Qur'an confirms, adds to, and reinterprets the Bible, thus returning to the pure revelation from which it was corrupted.

How Muslims understand the Qur'an

Muslims believe the Qur'an is the eternal, uncreated speech of God. The Qur'an describes itself as "a glorious Qur'an on a guarded tablet" (85:21-22). In other verses it is the Heavenly Tablet or The Mother of the Book. Again, we see the similarity between the Qur'an and the way in which Jesus is described in the Gospel of John. For Christians, Jesus is eternal, uncreated, and appears on earth at a particular point in human history. Muslims hold exactly the same view of the Qur'an; at a particular point in history, it comes down from heaven and enters our world, the transcendent entering history in a definitive act of what Christians call "salvation history."

As mentioned earlier, all Muslims commit to memory at least some of the Qur'an. Daily prayers always include the recitation of several verses, and these are recited without using a prayer book. Millions of Muslims around the world, however, memorize the entire Qur'an. This earns them the title of *hafiz* (guardian, or preserver), which comes from the same Arabic word in the Qur'an's description of itself as the "guarded tablet." Men and women who memorize the entire Qur'an usually begin as children in school, memorizing a few verses at a time. By the time they reach adolescence, they will have memorized the entire text of over 6,000 verses. Those who have children or have been around children know the gift that children have for memorization. For Muslims, this gift is best used when they give their children the Qur'an to memorize.

The physical text of the Qur'an has always been treated with great respect. Book printing came late to the Arab world, and it was not until the 18th century that Muslims began to use printed copies of the Qur'an. Prior to this, the Qur'an was copied by hand and often bound with elaborate hand-sewn bindings. It was not until the 20th century that cheap, mass-produced copies were available for Muslims. It is easy to see why the early Qur'an manuscripts would be treated with great care, for they were comparatively rare and valuable. However, the same care and respect is given to a cheap paperback copy of the Qur'an as it is to a priceless manuscript copy. This is because the text itself is considered to be the very Word of God. Devout Muslims will not handle a copy of the Qur'an without having gone through the same ablutions that allow them to be in a ritually pure state for the daily prayers (see Chapter Five). In devout homes, the Qur'an will be kept at the top of a shelf of books, and never in a spot where people might point their feet at it.

Observant Christians and Jews will find similar reverence in their own traditions. The host of the Catholic Eucharist, believed to be the body of Christ, is treated with tremendous respect after it is consecrated. In the Jewish tradition, the Torah scrolls are likewise handled with great joy and reverence. It should not be difficult to understand, therefore, why Muslims were so upset at the way in which the Qur'an was mistreated at Guantanamo Bay. Ask a Catholic how she would feel if the consecrated host had been urinated upon, or a Jew how he would feel if the Torah scroll had been kicked, and I suspect the reaction would be similar to Muslim reactions to the desecrations of the Qur'an. These analogies do not justify any violent response, of course, but they indicate the importance that sacred objects have among believers.

How readers of the Bible can read the Qur'an

Non-Muslim readers who are used to reading the Bible are sometimes mystified when they open a copy of the Qur'an. It reads very differently than does the Bible. Readers of the Bible are familiar with narrative, particularly the parables that Jesus tells to help people understand his teaching. In the Qur'an, it is often assumed that readers know the stories from the Bible; the Qur'an simply gives the true meaning of these stories. The Qur'an says, for example: "Recite to them in truth the story of the two sons of Adam" (5:27). The Qur'an does not name these sons, leaving it to the Islamic tradition to explain that they are Habeel (Abel) and Qabeel (Cain), whom Christians and Jews recognize from the book of Genesis.

The longest sustained narrative in the Qur'an is in Joseph (Chapter 12), which tells a story similar to the Genesis account of Joseph being sold into slavery by his brothers and his eventual return to his father Jacob. Other narratives are familiar to readers of the New Testament. Mary (Chapter 19), for example, tells the story of Gabriel's visit to Mary in almost exactly the same language as used in Luke's gospel. Readers who seek narrative in the Qur'an should begin with those chapters.

Most of the Qur'an, however, is not narrative. Surprisingly to many non-Muslims, the Qur'an is not primarily a law book, either. While it is true that shari'ah law (Islamic religious law) derives from the Qur'an, only about 300 of the Qur'an's more than 6,000 verses are explicitly legislative. Many of these verses were revealed at Medina, when the Muslim community began existing as a community and thus needed legal guidance.

Instead of narrative and law, much of the Qur'an is explicitly theological, with God speaking in the first person. This is important to Muslims, since they hear God speaking directly to them in the text. As a result, Muslims who are new to the Bible are sometimes mystified that it is often in the form of stories, and not the direct speech of God. They feel more at home when they read the direct speech of God found in parts of Exodus or in John's gospel. Muslim feminists, especially, also find it refreshing to hear God speaking directly to "believing women."

In reading the Qur'an, it is helpful for new readers to have an overall awareness of some of the themes that are discussed there. The late Fazlur Rahman, Pakistani scholar and professor of Islam at the University of Chicago, identified eight major themes in the Qur'an: God; humans as individuals; humans as members of a society; nature; revelation and prophets; eschatology; evil and Satan; and the emergence of the Muslim community. The themes that we have not yet touched on will be discussed in the next chapter. However, one more thematic undercurrent is worth mentioning here. For Muslims, it is not only human beings who are Muslim. The plants and the animals, the Qur'an tells us, are also Muslim, each one in their own way bowing to God. The trees bend down in the breeze, and birds spread their wings in prayer. Humans are unique in that they have a free choice of whether or not to obey and surrender to God.

To experience and understand the Qur'an, one should first hear it recited by a trained reciter – not try to read it. A number of Muslims are trained as professional reciters, as are cantors in the Jewish tradition. To hear them is to experience the Qur'an as it was first revealed – not as a book between two covers that is read with the eyes, but as an oral tradition to be heard through the ears.

If one is to begin with the written Qur'an, however, it is best to read the opening chapter first, and then the last 30 chapters or so.[1] Then, having tasted the language and style of the Qur'an, one can move on to the earlier, longer chapters. But be warned that the text is not straightforward in its style. Sometimes a chapter begins with a story, and other times stories are interspersed throughout. Sometimes God speaks in the first person singular, "I," and sometimes in the first person plural, "we" or "us." This royal we does not mean a plurality of gods, of course, since God is one; it is used to denote God's power and majesty. Sometimes, God is spoken of in the third person, always with the masculine pronoun he. This does not indicate a male gender for God; there is simply no neuter gender in Arabic as there is in some languages.

Commentaries

Given the divine origin of the Qur'an, it is not surprising that commentaries on the text are also important for Muslims. As in Judaism, where it is a given that religious leaders know the sacred text by heart, what distinguishes Muslim leaders the most is the number of commentaries that they know. Like Jewish commentaries on the Torah, Muslim commentaries on the Qur'an can be voluminous. Some may be as short as one or two volumes, but longer commentaries run to ten volumes or more. Commentators examine the text of the Qur'an line by line, and in some cases word by word. On rare occasions they go letter by letter in order to determine the meaning of the text. The Arabic word that describes the process is *tafseer*, which means "unveiling," even though it is understood that only God can uncover the pure meaning of the text.

Commentary on the Qur'an began in the eighth century, and became codified by the tenth century. Given the many contexts of Muslim life and thought through the ages, there is a wide diversity among commentaries. Sunnis and Shi'as have different commentary traditions that reflect their different understandings of Islam. Some commentaries are very old, while others are modern. Some work with grammatical, linguistic, or rhetorical analysis, while others seek hidden or metaphorical meanings. Especially in our day, some are explicitly political in their interpretations of the text.

Violence in the Qur'an

Many Jewish and Christian readers perceive the Qur'an to be a book of violence, while Muslim readers see it as a book of peace. While the Qur'an – like the Bible – does speak of the wrath of God, it overwhelmingly affirms the mercy of God. God says, for example, "My punishment is for whom I choose, but my mercy encompasses all things" (7:156). This echoes a hadith in which Muhammad quotes God as saying, "My mercy takes precedence over my wrath." The word *mercy* occurs in 181 verses of a standard English translation of the Qur'an, but the word *wrath* occurs only 64 times. If one expands the search to include *merciful* and *wrathful*, the difference becomes even more apparent: 307 to 66.

It is important to acknowledge that we probably know the contexts of our own scriptures much better than those of other peoples' holy books. We can read the book of Joshua, for example, and justify its violence by saying that it was appropriate for an earlier time, but not for our time. Or we can say that when Jesus says, "Think not that I am come to send peace on earth: I came not to send peace but a sword" (Matthew 10:34) – he is talking about societal divisions and disruptions, not physical violence. Similarly, the violence of the Book of Revelation is an eschatological violence to come. In the same way, Muslims often contextualize the violence found in the Qur'an. (See Chapter Six for a fuller discussion of violence.)

Experiencing the Qur'an through recitation and calligraphy

For Muslims, the Qur'an is not meant simply to be read. Many men and women are proficient in the art of *reciting* the Qur'an. There are a number of accepted styles in which the Qur'an is recited, with differences in melody, register, and pacing. Qur'an recitation is often done in the mosque, but it also occurs in the home, or in private religious ceremonies. With the advent of modern technology, Muslims can download the most famous reciters into their MP3 players, or listen to complete recitations on CD or DVD.

Muslims will often hold competitions to see who can best recite the Qur'an. The winners receive great recognition within in the Muslim world. While all of the reciters use the Arabic original, many of the best ones are not native speakers of Arabic. In the past few years, Indonesian reciters have won prizes in many competitions. There are also several famous female reciters of the Qur'an.

In addition to reciting and hearing the Qur'an, Muslims also experience it through calligraphy. Many Muslims will have verses or short chapters of the Qur'an displayed in their homes. These may be inexpensive reproductions, or priceless original works of calligraphy. They may be written in ink on paper, painted on cloth or ceramic tiles, or engraved in metal. One also sees Qur'anic calligraphy decorating the inside and outside of mosques.

Portrait of a calligrapher

Mohamed Zakariya is one of the finest Islamic calligraphers in the world, and has pioneered the art form in the United States. He first encountered Islamic calligraphy as a boy, while walking past an Armenian carpet store in Los Angeles. Then, in his late teens, he travelled in Morocco, where he became fascinated with Islam and Islamic calligraphy. Upon his return to the United States, he converted to Islam.

He returned on other journeys to North Africa and the Middle East, and studied manuscripts in the British Museum in London. In 1988, Zakariya received a diploma from the Turkish master calligrapher Hasan Celebi at the Research Center for Islamic History, Art and Culture in Istanbul, the first American to achieve this honour.

Today Zakariya lives with his family in Arlington, Virginia. His work has been displayed in various museums and galleries, and is in a number of private collections. He wrote the brochure *Music for the Eyes: An Introduction to Islamic and Ottoman Calligraphy* for an exhibit which toured America from 1998 to 2000, sponsored by the Los Angeles County Museum of Art and the Metropolitan Museum of Art. He was also commissioned by the United States Postal Service to design a 2001 stamp with calligraphy for "eid mubarak," the greeting ("a blessed celebration") Muslims use at Eid festivals. Mohamed Zakariya's work shows that American Islam has become an integral part of the Muslim world. Instead of American Muslims going to the Islamic world to study calligraphy, students from the Muslim world come to the United States to study with an American master.

5

Surrender to God: Muslim faith and life

Richard Thompson is one of the most accomplished guitar players in the world. Born in Britain, he was a founding member of the folk-rock group Fairport Convention. After Thompson left Fairport, he recorded with his first wife Linda; their last record, 1982's *Shoot Out the Lights*, received extensive critical acclaim. In the 1980s, Richard remarried and moved to southern California, where he continues to live. In 2006, he won a lifetime achievement award for folk music from the British Broadcasting Corporation.

To the surprise of many who enjoy his music, Thompson has been a Muslim since the 1970s. Like many Western converts, he found his way to the faith through Sufism, the mystical tradition in Islam. "Music is spiritual stuff," he once said in an interview, "and even musicians who clearly worship money, or fame, or ego, cannot help but express a better part of themselves sometimes when performing, so great is the gift of music, and so connected to our higher selves. What we believe informs everything we do, and music is no exception."

There is a common misconception among North Americans that music is forbidden in Islam. Unfortunately, some Muslims are guilty of spreading this notion; certain fundamentalist regimes have indeed placed restrictions on musicians. But the number of important Muslim musicians, such as Mos Def, Everlast, Cat Stevens (Yusuf Islam), Danny Thompson, Youssou N'Dour, Art Blakey, and Ali Touré give the lie to the notion that such restrictions are the norm. Anyone who has spent time in rural parts of the Muslim world, from Mali to Egypt to Turkey to Iran to Pakistan, knows the importance of music to Muslim village life.

A hadith of the Prophet Muhammad quotes him as saying, "God is beautiful and loves beauty." For most Muslims, music is one way of celebrating the beauty of God, while art is another way. In April of 2006, the second annual God Loves Beauty festival was hosted jointly by the Islamic Center of Southern California and St. James' Episcopal Church of Los Angeles. This festival was held over two days, one day devoted to visual arts, and another to the performing arts. As a participant, I particularly appreciated the young Muslim musicians from Los Angeles who, through their music, were able to express their joy at being Muslims. Their collaboration with young Christian musicians was a wonderful example of new forms of interfaith dialogue. For many Muslims, it is the continuing attempt at doing what is beautiful that is at the heart of Muslim life. This attitude underlies the core beliefs and practices of Muslims, which this chapter tries to outline.

Muslim life: the hadith of Gabriel

The textbook that I use for my introductory course on Islam is *The Vision of Islam* by Sachiko Murata and William C. Chittick.

One of the many reasons I like the book is that it uses Muslim categories to explain Islam. The book is framed around a famous story, "The Hadith of Gabriel," which begins the section on faith in one of the standard collections of hadiths.

The narrative is set in Medina, where a number of people are gathered around the Prophet Muhammad. Into their midst comes a mysterious stranger, who bears no mark of having travelled to arrive at the oasis town. The stranger calls Muhammad by his given name instead of his title, Messenger of God, and places his hands on Muhammad, indicating a close personal relationship between them.

The stranger asks Muhammad to tell him about Islam. Muhammad responds that Islam means bearing witness that there is no God but God and that Muhammad is the messenger of God; performing prayer; giving to charity; fasting during the month of Ramadan; and making the pilgrimage to Mecca if one has the financial means to do so. When Muhammad finishes, the man tells him that he is correct. Clearly, the companions of Muhammad are puzzled that a stranger would ask the Messenger of God about Islam and then tell Muhammad that his answers were correct. However, Muhammad seems not to be perplexed.

The man then asks Muhammad to explain faith. Muhammad replies that faith means believing in God; in God's angels; in God's books; in God's messengers; in the Day of Judgment; and in the measuring out of God's justice. Again, the man tells Muhammad that he is correct. The man asks the Prophet to tell him about doing what is beautiful. Muhammad replies that doing what is beautiful means that you worship God as if you see God – for even if you do not see God, God sees you.

The man then asks Muhammad to tell him about the Hour of Judgment following the Resurrection. Muhammad refuses to answer this question, saying that he knows no more about it than the man does. The man persists, and asks the Prophet to tell him some of the signs that mark the Hour of Judgment. Muhammad responds with what seems like a strange answer, telling the man that the Hour of Judgment will be marked by slave girls giving birth to their masters, and barefoot, destitute shepherds competing to erect magnificent buildings. After this, the mysterious stranger turns around and leaves. Muhammad waits for a while, then tells the people that the stranger was not a man, but the angel Gabriel who had come to teach them their religion.

This story speaks to Muslims about the truth of their religion. The teachings that Muhammad has brought are confirmed in the supernatural elements of the angel's visit: his sudden appearance bearing no signs of travel; his close familiarity with Muhammad; and his authority in the conversation. Muhammad's response to the trick question about the final judgment also indicates Muhammad's familiarity with God's mysterious values, which defy conventional logic. In any case, the four questions that Gabriel asked are at the heart of what it means to be Muslim. Let us examine each in turn.

Surrender: the Five Pillars of Islam

The first question Gabriel asks Muhammad is about the meaning of *Islam*. Literally, the term means "surrender" or "submission to God." However, this is not a passive submission; it is an engaged response to God. Muhammad's response to the angel revolves around five activities known as the Five Pillars of Islam. Like Judaism, Islam is a religion of orthopraxy (right conduct). By comparison, many Christians believe that all the good conduct in the world will not save a person; what is most important is orthodoxy (right belief). Belief in Jesus as the Christ is at the heart of salvation. Muslims and Jews, to be sure, also have an understanding of what is right belief, but they are more concerned with the performance of actions. Some of the Five Pillars are activities that some Muslims may never be able to do – such as the pilgrimage to Mecca if they cannot afford it, or fasting if they have a health condition that precludes it – even though it remains an ideal. Others, such as prayer, are repeated throughout the day, and are standard practices for everyone.

Another important feature of the Five Pillars is their emphasis on community. Muslims refer to their *ummah* in much the same way that Christians speak of the church as a body of believers. The Prophet Muhammad said that anyone who performs the prayers and eats the ritually acceptable food is a Muslim. While these activities are sometimes done in private, Muslims assume that they are essentially communal. Muslims value the idea of corporate worship, just as Jews and Christians do. While it is perfectly acceptable to pray at home alone, it is better to pray with others. While it is acceptable to break your fast alone, it is better to do it with others. The pilgrimage and the giving to charity are by definition, in community.

Keeping in mind the importance of active faith in the context of the *ummah*, let us examine each of the Pillars in turn:

1. Witness (*shahadah*), or faith statement. The Muslim confession of faith is one sentence in two parts: "I bear witness that there is no God but God, and I bear witness that Muhammad is the Messenger of God." The only ritual that marks one's conversion to Islam is the recitation of this faith statement, with sincerity, in the presence of Muslim witnesses. Observant Muslims will recite the faith statement numerous times throughout the day in their daily prayers.

The first part of the faith statement indicates the monotheism of Islam. There is no one worthy of worship other than the one true God. Muslims believe this to be the same God that Jews, Christians, and other monotheists worship. According to one hadith, the Prophet Muhammad said that all children are born with this true faith; it is the parents who turn them into Jews, Christians, Zoroastrians, or Muslims. The second part of the faith statement indicates the importance of Muhammad. A number of times in the Qur'an, Muslims are commanded to obey both God and Muhammad. "Obey God and the Messenger that you might find mercy" (3:132). For Muslims, Muhammad is the example to follow in the observance of the Five Pillars.

2. Prayer (*salat*). The daily prayers are of primary importance to Muslims, reminding them that all people and all created things are to praise God and surrender to God. Muslims embody this attitude in their postures of prayer as they stand, bow, and prostrate themselves, symbolizing their submission before God. The Arabic word *masjid*, or "place of prostration," is used to describe a Muslim house of prayer, also known as a mosque. While congregational prayer at a house of prayer is always preferred, one can pray in any clean place. However, noon prayer on Fridays is communal. It is obligatory for all men to attend, but optional for women.

Observant Muslims are required to pray five times a day, facing the direction of the Ka'ba in Mecca, the first place of monotheistic prayer. Before the prayers begin, Muslims should be in a state of ritual purity, accomplished through the washing of hands, face (including mouth and nostrils), arms, and feet. A full bath ablution is required after activities, such as sexual intercourse, that leave one in a state of ritual impurity. Women are required to have their heads covered for prayer, while this head covering is optional for men. Both men and women are required to dress modestly.

If two or more people are praying, then one person stands slightly in front and leads the prayer. This person is the imam, or prayer leader. A woman can lead a group of women in prayer, but a man traditionally leads a group of men or a mixed gender group (although, as Chapter Seven indicates, that protocol has been breached in North America). In congregational prayer, men and women, separated by gender, line up in rows behind the imam. In many mosques there are separate prayer areas for women.[1]

The five daily prayer times are in the morning; at noon; in the afternoon; in the evening; and at night. While the Muslim religious calendar is lunar, daily prayer times are determined by the movement of the sun. Morning prayer takes place between dawn and sunrise. Noon prayer occurs soon after the sun has reached its peak in the sky. Afternoon prayer is between noon prayer and sunset. Evening prayer takes place after sunset. Finally, night prayer occurs between the evening prayer and dawn. Each of these prayer times consists of a fixed number of cycles of standing, bowing, and kneeling – two cycles in the morning, four at noon, four in the afternoon, three in the evening, and four prayer cycles at night. At Friday congregational prayers, two short sermons take the place of two of the four prayer cycles. These sermons are usually given by the person who leads the prayer.

A prayer time begins with a call to prayer (*adhan*). Traditionally, this is broadcast outside the mosque, to let people in the community know that it is time for prayer. In North America, however, noise restrictions in many communities require that Muslims make the call inside the mosque, to those who are already assembled for the prayer. The call, translated from the Arabic, says:

> God is Greater (repeated four times)
> I bear witness that there is no god but God (repeated twice)
> I bear witness that Muhammad is the Messenger of God (repeated twice)
> Come alive to the prayer (repeated twice)
> Come alive to the good (repeated twice)
> God is Greater (repeated twice)
> There is no god but God.

In the morning, "Prayer is better than sleep" is added after the line "Come alive to the good." The prayers are then recited in Arabic. They consist of the first chapter of the Qur'an, along with other short verses or chapters of the Qur'an as chosen by the person leading the prayer. After the formal prayer, one can make one's own personal prayer to God, in whatever language one chooses.

3. Charity (*zakat*). The Qur'an frequently links prayer with charitable giving. Wealth is seen as a blessing from God, and Muslims who have wealth are expected to care for those who are in need. Christianity and Judaism speak of "tithes and offerings"; In Islam, such giving is referred to as *zakat* (purification, or increase), the charity that is obligatory for all adults who have more than the minimum amount of certain assets. That minimum is currently set at the equivalent of about US $1,500 in gold and silver, savings (bank accounts, stocks, bonds), livestock or agricultural produce, goods for sale, and rental income. Each year, Muslims are obligated to calculate how much wealth they have in addition to the standard minimum, and to give 2.5 percent of that sum for charitable purposes. In addition to *zakat*, many Muslims voluntarily perform other charity, described in the Qur'an as offering a "loan to God" (2:245). This can include the feeding of the hungry, contributing to a hospital, or even smiling at your neighbour.

Traditionally, those eligible to receive the *zakat* include a variety of people: the poor and needy; those who administer the charity; recent converts or potential converts who need financial support; slaves in earlier eras who needed money to buy their freedom; those in debt; or needy travellers. The money could also go to "the cause of God," – a general term from the Qur'an that Muslims interpret in many ways. Those who receive the money must use it as intended; they may not pass it on to other causes or to other people, including one's immediate family. The voluntary charity, of course, may be given to anyone, Muslim or not.

4. Fasting (*sawm*) in the month of Ramadan. As mentioned earlier, the Muslim religious calendar is lunar. Each of the 12 months extends from new moon to new moon, a period of 29 or 30 days. On average, the lunar calendar year has about 354 days, 11 days shorter than in the solar calendar. In the Jewish calendar, which is also lunar, a "leap month" is added every few years to keep the lunar calendar synchronized with the solar calendar. The Qur'an forbids such synchronization; in the Muslim calendar the solar calendar simply cycles alongside the lunar one. Each year, therefore, important Muslim holidays will be about 11 days earlier than they were in the previous solar year.

The most important part of the Muslim calendar is the ninth month, Ramadan, when all able adults are required to fast during daylight hours. The fast means a complete break from eating, drinking (not even water), smoking, or sexual activity from dawn to sunset. When Ramadan falls during winter months in the Northern hemisphere, the dawn to sunset period is not long. However, over the years the time of the fast will increase as the days get longer during the summer months. In extreme latitudes where the sun does not set in the summer and rise in the winter, Muslims are to follow a schedule that parallels the fasting schedule of Muslims in Mecca.

There is no set age at which one begins the fast. School age children may begin by fasting a day or two during Ramadan, increasing a day or two every year as the child gets older. By adolescence, many Muslims are fasting for the entire month. The fast is not meant to be harmful, so anyone whose health would be negatively affected is exempt. This includes small children, pregnant or nursing women, diabetics, people who are ill, travellers, people who are not mentally responsible for their own actions, and the elderly. Women who are menstruating are exempt from fasting, but they must later make up the days they missed.

During Ramadan, Muslims wake up before the dawn and eat a small meal. They then declare their intention to fast for the entire day. While some try to limit their physical activity during the month of fasting, they are expected to carry out their normal work duties. At sunset, they break the fast, preferably with a communal, ceremonial meal (*iftar*) before the evening prayer. In today's hectic world where every family member often has a different schedule, Ramadan is a time to intentionally take the time to break the fast together.

Ramadan is a spiritual month, and in many ways resembles the Jewish Sabbath. It is a time for rest, family fellowship, and spiritual reflection – only it lasts a month, not just a day. For 11 months out of the year, one makes one's way in the world. During the month of fasting, however, one reflects on the life of the spirit. Muslims are encouraged to spend more time reading the Qur'an, and to pray extra prayers at night. On certain nights at the end of Ramadan, devout Muslims spend the entire night in the mosque, praying to God. Ramadan ends with the large festival of Eid al-Fitr (the celebration of the breaking of the fast), a day of congregational prayer, exchanging of gifts and new clothes in families, and giving to charity. Before the beginning of this celebration, the head of each household must give a donation to charity.

Ramadan is thus seen as a disciplined way to practice surrender to God. One voluntarily gives up perfectly normal activities, such as eating and drinking. This can increase one's willpower to avoid negative behaviours such as getting angry, lying, or gossiping about others. This is the interior dimension of the fast – to make oneself more aware of God, and to be conscious that one is living in God's presence. The fasting also makes one thankful for the simple pleasures of food and water that God provides. Ramadan is a wonderful reminder of our dependence on the providence of God. In a world where fancy new restaurant menus and new coffee options multiply each week, there is something to be said for a glass of water and some dried fruit to break one's fast.

Fasting, like the works of charity that are performed at Ramadan, also connects Muslims to those who are hungry all the time. The message is clear: If one has felt physically what it means to be hungry and thirsty, then perhaps one is more inclined to work towards a world where no one is hungry and thirsty. In this way, Ramadan stresses the idea of community responsibility.

5. Pilgrimage (*hajj*) to Mecca. The last of the five pillars is incumbent upon all Muslims who have the financial resources to perform it: a pilgrimage (*hajj*) to Mecca during the month of pilgrimage, the 12th month of the Islamic calendar. Historically, this journey would often take several months or more by land travel, and could cost a lifetime of savings. Also, since one could die on the journey, one had to make sure that all of one's debts were paid before starting out. Since the 1980s, however, the vast majority of pilgrims have travelled by air, landing at a specially-constructed terminal at Jeddah's King Abdulaziz International Airport. The convenience of modern air travel and of this terminal (devoted exclusively to the *hajj*) has helped boost the number of pilgrims to some two million people every year. While this is a small fraction of the world's one billion Muslims, it requires tremendous organization.

Mecca itself is considered a sacred area, forbidden to non-Muslims. The rites of the pilgrims are not a secret, and are broadcast around the world by Saudi television each year and on many Muslim web pages. Still, the physical restriction of Mecca to the Muslim faithful bothers some in the modern, ecumenical age, leading some to disguise themselves as Muslims in order to travel to Mecca. The exclusivity, however, is similar to the way Mormons restrict entry to their temples to practising Mormons, or the way Roman Catholic churches serve communion only to Catholics.

The significance of Mecca revolves around the story of Ishmael. For Jews and Christians, Isaac is the son whom Abraham was willing to offer in sacrifice on Mount Moriah until God intervened and provided a ram instead (Genesis 22). For Muslims, however, that son was Ishmael, and the aborted sacrifice took place in Mecca. This is where Abraham and Ishmael built the first place of monotheistic prayer, the Ka'ba, also known as the House of God (Qur'an, 2:124–129). It is to Mecca that Ishmael and his mother, Hagar, came when Abraham's wife Sarah expelled them from Canaan. Here God revealed the well of Zamzam to provide water for Hagar and Ishmael, and which was later used to provide water for Muslim pilgrims.

The rituals for the pilgrimage are outlined in the Qur'an (22:26–29). Once the pilgrims arrive in Mecca, they don a simple white outfit that signifies their pilgrim status. This also hides their economic and cultural distinctions, showing that all are equal before God. Their first rituals upon arrival are to walk counter-clockwise around the Ka'ba to symbolize their commitment to the worship of one God, then to run between the two hills of Safa and Marwa to commemorate Hagar's frantic search for water for Ishmael.

The formal pilgrimage begins on the eighth day of the month of pilgrimage, when the pilgrims migrate, by bus or on foot, 20 kilometres east of Mecca to the plain of Arafat. On the way, some stop for the night at Mina. Once they reach the plain, the faithful perform the central ritual of the pilgrimage, the standing at Arafat. From noon to sunset they stand, praying and asking for the mercy of God. It is considered a sort of practice run for the Day of Judgement, when all of humanity will be resurrected and will stand before God. The plain is especially sacred because it was here that Muhammad gave his farewell sermon. It is also where the last verse of the Qur'an was revealed to him shortly before his death: "This day have I [God] perfected your religion for you, completed my favour upon you, and chosen for you Islam as a religion" (5:3).

From Arafat, the pilgrims return to Mecca, stopping at Muzdalifah. There, they pick up pebbles for a ritual to take place at Mina. According to Muslim tradition, Mina is where Abraham was commanded to sacrifice his son. In resistance to Satan's temptation to disobey God, Abraham threw stones at Satan to cast him away. To emulate Abraham's actions, the pilgrims throw stones at pillars that have been erected to represent Satan. Following this ceremonial stoning, the pilgrims offer an animal sacrifice – a lamb, goat, cow, or camel, depending on one's wealth – representing Abraham's sacrifice of the ram. This celebration of the sacrifice, known as Eid al-Adha, occurs on the tenth day of the month. The pilgrims then have their hair cut, walk around the Ka'ba, and finish the pilgrimage.

Shi'a variations

My description of the Five Pillars reflects the Sunni understanding and practice. Shi'a Muslims perform these same activities with slight variations:

- In their prayers, the Shi'as add the line "Come alive to the best of works" after "Come alive to the good." They also do not add "Prayer is better than sleep" to the morning prayer call.
- After the line "I bear witness that Muhammad is the Messenger of God" they may add the lines "I bear witness that Ali is the friend of God" and "I bear witness that Ali is the proof of God."

- Shi'as sometimes combine noon and afternoon prayers, and evening and night prayers, resulting in what looks like three prayers per day.
- Shi'as have slightly different postures in prayer, holding their hands in a different way, and touching their head to a baked piece of earth from Karbala rather than the prayer mat itself. (This is explained below in the discussion of the holiday of Ashura.) Ismaili Shi'a Muslims will pray in a different way altogether in their own places of prayer known as a *jamaatkhana* (house of meeting). Their worship includes the singing of devotional songs known as *ginans*.
- When it comes to the giving of charity, Shi'as give the same 2.5 percent of their wealth, but it may be given to their religious leader for distribution to the poor and needy. In addition, the Shi'a give an extra 20 percent of their net income to charity.
- During Ramadan, Shi'as wait until the sun has completely set before breaking the fast.
- Finally, after they complete the *hajj* Shi'a pilgrims may visit the tombs of their venerated Imams.

The six articles of faith (*iman*)

Gabriel's second request during his interrogation was: "Tell me, Muhammad, about faith." Muhammad responds by telling Gabriel the six things that Muslims are to believe. For Muslims, faith (*iman*) is self-commitment or understanding. It is an acceptance of the truth of what God commands. Faith therefore goes deeper than the actions of the Five Pillars; as we all know, one may do the right things for the wrong reasons. The Qur'an is clear on this distinction between actions and understanding.

It tells of a group of Bedouin who came to the Prophet to tell him that they had faith. God commanded Muhammad to respond thus to the Bedouin: "You [the Bedouin] do not have faith. Instead, [you should] say 'We have submitted,' for faith has not yet entered your hearts. If you obey God and God's messenger, God will not diminish anything from your actions" (Qur'an 49:14).

For Muslims, the heart is the organ of faith. As one hadith quotes the Prophet as saying, "Faith is a knowledge in the heart, a voicing with the tongue, and an activity with the limbs." For Muslims, having faith means to have an inner posture of thankfulness to God. This state is known as *shukr* in Arabic, and is contrasted with *kufr* (refusal) – the act of being ungrateful. The term for someone who does not have faith is *kaffir*, someone who says no to God. So the opposite of faith is not doubt or disbelief, but a lack of gratitude to God. People may be familiar with the term *infidel*, but it is important to remember that this is not a Muslim term for a non-Muslim; it is a Christian term for someone who is not of the faith.

The articles of faith that Muslims hold in their hearts are the following:

1. Oneness of God. For Muslims, the cardinal principle of faith is the oneness of God. In Arabic, this is known as *tawheed* (unity). Like Judaism and Christianity, Islam is monotheistic, and Muslims believe they worship the same God worshipped by Jews and Christians. Jews, Catholics, Orthodox Christians and Muslims have differences in their understanding of God, but none would confess to a plurality of gods. For Muslims, the greatest sin is to give anyone but God the status of God.

2. Angels. In our modern world, angels have made something of a comeback. Guardian angel pins and pictures of angels are everywhere. In the Muslim tradition there is no such comeback, because angels have never left. Muslims believe that God's angels surround us at all times, recording our deeds. The angels perform other functions as well, such as supporting the throne of God and bringing down God's blessings to the world.

When Muslims greet one another, they use an Arabic greeting regardless of the language they speak: "*Al-salaamu alaikum*, peace be upon you." The response is, "*Wa alaikum al-salaam*, and upon you, peace." Interestingly, "you" in the Arabic greeting is always plural, even when individuals greet each other. This is because one greets not only the person, but also the angels that accompany him or her. It is the same in prayer, which ends with the same greeting of peace whether or not one is praying in the congregation. The person thus greets the surrounding angels.

In these pages we have already met Gabriel, the angel of revelation. The Qur'an names others as well: the archangel Michael, and Harut and Marut, who taught in Babylon. In addition, the Muslim tradition speaks of Seraphiel, the angel who will blow the trumpet to signal the end of the world, and Azrael, the angel of death.

3. The revealed books. As described in Chapter Four, Muslims believe that God sent previous revelations before the Qur'an. These included a text given to Abraham that is now believed to be lost; the Torah given to Moses; the Psalms given to David; and the Gospel given to Jesus. For Muslims, all of these texts were later altered, and none of them exist today with the same content that was revealed to the respective prophets. As a result of alterations in these earlier texts, the Qur'an was sent down as the final revelation. As such, Muslims use only the text of the Qur'an for liturgical purposes. The hadith literature is of secondary importance for Muslims; it contains the words of Muhammad, not the very Word of God. Muslims may read and find value in the Hebrew Bible and the New Testament, but these are not considered religiously authoritative texts for them. In much the same way, one would never have a reading from the Qur'an as an official part of a Catholic liturgy.

4. Messengers and prophets. For Muslims, Muhammad is the last in a long line of prophets. The Qur'an names a number of these prophets and refers to 124,000 others that have been sent, each speaking the language of the people to whom they were sent. Jonah is one such prophet, honoured also by Christians and Jews, who was sent to warn a particular community. Messengers are a smaller group of prophets who are given a specific message, and the Muslim tradition identifies over 300 of these. Five of these (Abraham, Moses, David, Jesus, and Muhammad) are given an actual text. Other messengers are given a universal law to bring not only to their community, but to all of humanity. Noah, for example, is seen as a messenger because, according to Muslim tradition, he receives laws about diet and marriage to pass on to all people.

5. The "Hour of Judgment." In Gabriel's interrogation, Muhammad has very little to say about the events of the last day, which includes the Hour of Judgment. Muslims share with Jews and Christians a similar notion of eschatology (last things). Just as there was a first day of creation, so there will be a last day of history. Sunni Muslims believe that Jesus will return to lead the final battle between good and evil. For Shi'a Muslims, it is the Hidden Imam who will return as the Mahdi or divinely guided one. All Muslims believe, however, that everyone will be resurrected in the end, and will give account before God.

6. The justice of God At the Hour of Judgment, or the Day of Resurrection, people will get what they deserve. Those who deserve punishment and hell for their wrongdoing will earn it, while those who deserve paradise as their reward will receive it. Muslims, like Jews and Christians, have questions about the afterlife. Who will God assign to heaven, and who to hell? Will God who is merciful really punish people eternally with hell? Will everyone eventually get to heaven? The answers to all of these questions are known only to God.

Doing what is beautiful (*ihsan*)

Gabriel's third question of Muhammad is about doing what is beautiful. Muhammad answers that doing what is beautiful means that you worship God as if you see God. This takes us into the realm of intentionality. For Muslims, the intent behind an act is more important than the act itself. A woman may intend to go to evening prayer at the mosque, for example, but her car won't start. Her prayer at home is better than the conduct of a woman who does make it to the mosque, but goes only to impress someone. The importance of intent in the performance of religious duties is symbolized in the statement with which Muslims begin each day during Ramadan: "I intend to fast this day during the month of Ramadan."

This intention of the heart is closely related to a quality that, according to the Qur'an, Muslims should seek: *taqwa*, which translates best as "awareness of God." God says: "O humankind! Truly We created you from a single male and female, and made you into tribes and nations that you might know each other. Truly the most honoured of you in the sight of God is the one with the most awareness of God [*taqwa*]. Truly God is All-Knowing, Aware" (49:13).

Unfortunately, as in all religious communities, there are too many Muslims who take upon themselves the judgment of how others reflect or don't reflect this quality – as if they have access to a special sort of "*taqwa* meter" that can measure the amount of piety in someone's heart. As the Qur'an clearly points out, it is God alone who has full knowledge of the piety that a person has, and God alone who decides the rewards and punishments that we will receive. I try to reflect such a suspension of judgment in my classes when I distribute a list of web pages about Muslim groups in North America. The disclaimer that I include at the top of the page reads: "This list includes various groups who consider themselves to be Muslim. I make no judgment about their Islam, but I understand that other Muslims may be all too willing to do this." The list includes links to gay and lesbian Muslim support groups, which many Muslims think is incompatible with Islam. It also includes links to Ahmadiyya and Ismaili communities, which some Muslims think are outside of Islam. All of these groups, of course, think of themselves as Muslim.

Since Muslims try to be conscious of pleasing God in all that they do, awareness of God is at the core of the faith. This resonates deeply with the words on the seal of the Jesuit university where I teach: *Ad Majorem Dei Gloriam*, "for the greater glory of God." In Islam, God-awareness is expressed in everyday acts of worship, but also in the creation of extraordinary art. The importance of calligraphy was highlighted in the last chapter. Among the mystics, the language of poetry is the art form of choice (see Chapter Eight). The architecture of mosques and Muslim mausoleums is particularly well-known; perhaps the most beautiful building in the world is the Taj Mahal, a mausoleum built by an Indian Muslim ruler. Muslim visual art also appears in paintings, textiles, and ceramics, and is displayed in many fine coffee-table books.

Islamic festivals

All Muslims celebrate two major festivals, or *eids*: Eid al-Fitr and Eid al-Adha. Both are great celebrations of congregational prayer, feasting, and giving to charity. During the festivals, Muslims greet each other with the words *eid mubarak*, "may you have a blessed celebration." Eid al-Fitr marks the end of the month of Ramadan and begins on the first day of the following month. It is marked by as large a congregational prayer service as possible. In Muslim countries, some mosques can hold thousands of people for just such an occasion, much like the great cathedrals of Europe. In North America, Muslims have no such large mosques, so they rent facilities such as the Toronto Skydome or the Los Angeles Convention Center for the occasion.

The second is Eid al-Adha, which commemorates Abraham offering up his son for sacrifice. This is celebrated on the tenth day of the month of pilgrimage. Traditionally, the head of the household slaughters an animal, and the meat is eaten and distributed to the poor. These days, when many live in cities and have no access to animals – nor the skill to slaughter an animal – Muslims often rely on commercial butchers to do the slaughtering for them.

Many Muslims also celebrate the Mawlid, the birthday of the Prophet Muhammad. For some, the singing of devotional songs about the Prophet are part of the festivities. Other Muslims, however, frown on this practice, believing that it puts too much emphasis on Muhammad and takes away from the glory of God. They fear that it may become a holiday like Christmas, which has become more about commercialism than the birth of Jesus.

In addition to these two festivals, Shi'a Muslims observe Ashura on the tenth day of the Month of Muharram in the Islamic calendar. It commemorates the martyrdom of Hussain, the third Imam for Shi'as. This is clearly not a holiday of celebration, but one of sorrow and remembrance, just as Good Friday is for Christians. Shi'a Muslims will tell the story of the martyrdom of Hussain through a kind of passion play, where a white horse without a rider symbolizes the fallen Hussain. As mentioned earlier, when Shi'a Muslims pray, they use a disc of pressed clay from Karbala, Iraq, where the very blood of Hussain was spilled. So the death of Hussain is remembered each time one's forehead touches the earth in prayer.

Shari'ah: Islamic religious law

No discussion about Muslim beliefs and practices would be complete without a discussion of Islamic law. For Muslims, the law is of fundamental importance, since Islam does not distinguish between religious and civil law as do most Western societies. Under shari'ah law, acts of worship, marriage and divorce, inheritance, and the buying and selling of goods are all covered under the same legal system. The literal meaning of the Arabic word *shari'ah* is "the road to water." The word finds parallels in other religious traditions. Jews refer to religious law as *halacha* (the path one walks). First Nations people refer to "the Red Road" as the path one should follow in living respectfully in creation. Similarly to live by shari'ah is to "walk it like you talk it" – to live according to the principles of Islam.

The roots of law. As in other legal traditions, Muslims distinguish between the law, and the principles by which people codify and interpret the law. Shari'ah is the law, and *fiqh* is jurisprudence, the sciences of determining the application of the law. There are traditionally four sources of jurisprudence: the Qur'an; the tradition of the Prophet Muhammad (*sunnah*); the use of analogies (*qiyas*); and community consensus (*ijma'*).

The Qur'an is the supreme source of law for Muslims, since they consider it to be the very Word of God. While the Qur'an does contain laws, however, it is not a legal manual, but it has played a significant role in shaping shari'ah law. The second source, the example of the Prophet Muhammad, is the information found in the hadiths or sayings of Muhammad, which are central to the *sunnah*, or tradition. From the hadiths, religious scholars have collected and ordered many of the precise instructions that Muslims are to follow regarding prayer, fasting, greetings, or commercial transactions.

The third source of law for jurists has been analogical reasoning. If there was a new problem facing jurists, they would search for an analogy to something that was described in either the Qur'an or the *sunnah*. This automatically has led to differences of opinion among jurists as to what is analogous to what, and how far that analogy could be carried. To mention but one example, neither the Qur'an nor the traditions about Muhammad have anything to say about illegally downloading music on your computer, or purchasing pirated copies of DVDs.

However, for modern jurists, these are analogous to the theft of property in Muhammad's time.

The fourth source is the principle of consensus. The Prophet once said, "My community will not agree on an error." As with the principle of analogy, there is even more discussion and debate about this fourth source. Who determines consensus – the religious scholars or the larger community? Is the consensus in one time and place legally binding on those in another time and place?

The schools of law. Given these four different sources of law, there is no one legal system that all Muslims follow. There are four accepted Sunni schools of law, one major legal school for the Imami Shi'a community, and unique schools of law for other Shi'as. These schools are named after their founding jurists. The four Sunni schools, all established in the eighth and ninth centuries are the Hanafi (founded by Abu Hanifa); Maliki (Malik ibn Anas); Shafi'i (Muhammad al-Shafi'i); and Hanbali (Ahmad ibn Hanbal). The Imami Shi'a school is the Ja'fari, founded by the sixth Imam, Ja'far al-Sadiq, who died in 765. The schools differ in the amount and type of analogical reasoning and consensus that they allow. The Maliki and Hanafi schools are more liberal in these respects, while the Hanbali school is the most conservative.

Islamic ethics. Islamic ethical behaviour is quite nuanced. There are five categories of conduct into which actions are divided: required; commended; neutral; not recommended; and prohibited. The first category includes actions which are rewarded when performed and punished when not performed. These are actions that are obligatory for all Muslims, such as the Five Pillars described in this chapter. The second category consists of acts that are not obligatory but recommended. Giving more than the minimum to charity, for example, is encouraged but not required. The third category is acts that are neutral and left to personal choice. These individual decisions could include choosing to fly to a business meeting rather than taking the train, or opting for grapefruit rather than apple juice at breakfast.

The fourth category is acts that are objectionable but not prohibited. Divorce, for example, is allowed in the Muslim tradition, but only as a last resort if the marriage has failed. The final category is acts which are prohibited and are punishable under shari'ah law. These would include stealing, drinking alcohol, or using any type of intoxicating drugs. Under shari'ah law, some crimes are punishable that are no longer criminalized under North American law. However, there is still flexibility in the application and interpretation of laws in the Muslim world. The death penalty, for example, is an option for the crime of murder, but the family of the murder victim has the right to decide if the murderer should be put to death.

Dietary laws. Muslims use the term halal for the food that is permitted to them. This parallels the Jewish use of the term kosher for food that is acceptable in the Jewish tradition. Certain kinds of food, such as pork, alcohol, carrion, blood, or any meat that has been sacrificed to anyone other than God is forbidden. As with kosher, halal food is food that has been prepared in the acceptable manner. To be considered halal, beef, for example, must be appropriately prepared. A prayer must be offered before the animal is killed; the animal must be killed as humanely as possible; and as much blood as possible must be drained from the animal, since consumption of blood is forbidden. As the number of Muslims grows, more and more halal food products are available in North America. If one is not able to find a halal butcher, however, Muslim jurists allow the faithful to use kosher meat as the next best alternative.

PART TWO

Issues for Dialogue

6

Violence and jihad

Before the terrorist attacks of September 11, 2001, I would begin my courses on Islam with biographies of the Prophet Muhammad. I used a critical historical biography written by a non-Muslim, as well as a standard biography that told the story in the way Muslims understood it. This allowed us to compare the Muhammad of history with the Holy Prophet of the Muslim faithful. I did this because prior to 9-11, my students had little knowledge about Islam. The non-Muslim students were eager to learn, and the Muslim students wanted to know more about their own tradition because they had never studied it before.

In January of 2002, when I taught my first post-9-11 class on Islam, I realized that this approach would no longer work. The students were no longer ignorant about Islam. Unfortunately, however, almost all the information they had was wrong. Since almost all of their information came from the media and not from contact with actual Muslims or scholars of Islam, I used a small book written by Neil Postman and Steve Powers called *How to Watch TV News*. The book exposed a common misconception among my students that television news tells the truth – when in fact it is often driven by a demand for entertainment value, ratings, and advertising income. In our discussions, my students agreed with me that the news parody delivered on the television comedy program *The Daily Show with Jon Stewart* was actually better informed than any other newscast.

Since most North Americans rely on television for their knowledge of world events, misleading information about Islam and Muslim lives is common. As a result, common perceptions are that Islam promotes violence, is more violent than any other religion, and oppresses women (a topic that will be addressed in Chapter Seven). I am especially amazed that North Americans get their information from people who are not Muslim, who know very little about Islam, and who in some cases have a blatant anti-Muslim bias. Most of us would not trust a Holocaust denier to give us an account of the tragedy of the Holocaust. We might be suspicious of a liberal Protestant telling us what evangelical Protestants believe, especially if that person was publicly biased against evangelicals. Yet we will listen to a talk show host who knows nothing about the Qur'an or about how it is understood in Muslim religious life tell us that it is a book of violence.

Authors have made a great deal of money writing inflammatory books about Islam, academics have made careers out of the "clash of civilizations" thesis, television commentators have repeated the lie that Muslims have not condemned violence and terrorism, and religious leaders have described Islam as an "evil and wicked religion." In this chapter, I hope to bring some balance and clarity to a number of realities that seem to attract a great deal of misunderstanding: (1) the very serious issues of violence in Islam (including recent Muslim violence); (2) the abhorrence that many Muslims have of violence; (3) stereotypes of Islam and Muslims as inherently violent; and (4) the larger context of violence in our world (not just the Muslim world), much of which is woven into the fabric of our society in such a way that we may not even regard it as our own violence.

Sorting out the vocabulary

To begin to explore the truth about the place of violence in Islam, it is fitting to begin with a word that has made its way into our English vocabulary, but is almost always misunderstood. The word *jihad*, often mistranslated as "holy war," appears only four times in the Qur'an. The verb form of the word, *jahada*, occurs about 25 times, while *mujahid* (one who makes jihad) appears another four times. The verb means to strive or struggle in the path of God, and the noun refers to that same struggle. The term for war is *harb*; "holy war," therefore, would be *harb muqaddas*. Those who wage war against society or fight such a war would be *muharibun*, a word that will be discussed below.

The Muslim tradition has distinguished between two types of jihad, the inner and the outer struggle in the path of God. The inner jihad is the personal struggle to become a better Muslim, and has nothing to do with war and violence. The mystics are especially good at understanding this inner struggle, as discussed in Chapter Eight. The struggle is familiar to people of any religion who try to temper inclinations toward evil with an ongoing commitment to righteousness. It is the Christian who asks herself what Jesus would do and tries to follow suit. It is the Jew who makes a contribution to charity rather than spend the money on himself. Similarly, it is the Muslim who fasts, and in her fast seeks to abstain from anger or spite against her fellow human beings. All are engaged in an inner jihad.

The outer jihad is the effort to make one's society reflect the principles of submission to God. In this way, it can best be described not as any sort of violent struggle, but as what Christians refer to as bearing faithful witness, living your faith in such a way as to affect the structures of society. The Prophet Muhammad said that the greatest jihad is to speak the truth to an unjust ruler. Sadly, some Muslims have understood outer jihad to be a struggle against Jews and Christians, citing Jews and Christians as unbelievers. However, I think this misses the meanings of the terms *belief* and *unbelief*. When the Qur'an addresses itself to believers, it is not speaking only to Muslims. The Qur'an is explicit here: "whoever believes in God and the Day of Judgment and does good, they shall have no fear, neither shall they grieve" (5:69). A believer is one who believes in the one true God and is thankful to God, whether Muslim, Jew, or Christian. Unbelievers, by definition, are not non-Muslims, but those who are not thankful to God.

Muslims commonly use the term *jihadists* for those who engage in this outer struggle with violence. In the 1980s, North American Christians, who have their own definitions of a "just war," did not necessarily consider this a bad thing. That was when the American government helped to arm the Afghan *mujahideen* (the plural of *mujahid*, or one who makes jihad) against the the Soviet Union, which had invaded Afghanistan in 1979. The mujahideen at that time were famously described by President Ronald Reagan as "freedom fighters." Tragically, through American military and economic support, these same people would become the Taliban who, two decades later, would be ousted by their former supporters, the Americans.

Many North Americans today confuse the mujahideen with "terrorists." The latter are described by a term that Muslim legal scholars use: *muharibun* (those who make war against society). Khaled Abou El Fadl, one of the most brilliant Muslim legal scholars in North America, explores the muharibun in his book *The Great Theft: Wrestling Islam from the Extremists.* "The classical jurists, nearly without exception," he writes, "argued that those who attack by stealth, while targeting noncombatants in order to terrorize the resident and wayfarer, are corrupters of the earth...; those guilty of this crime were considered enemies of humankind and were not to be given quarter or sanctuary anywhere." It is clear, therefore, that the Muslim tradition itself distinguishes between those who struggle to make their society more Islamic, including those who engage in a "just war," and those who destroy society through terrorism and violence.

War and violence in the life of Muhammad and in the Qur'an

Beyond the Arabic terms, however, an understanding of the place of war and violence in Islam should begin with the life and times of the Prophet Muhammad. As described in Chapter Three, Muhammad was born into a tribal and polytheistic world. Gross inequalities among people defined the society, and slavery was an accepted part of the historical milieu (as it was in Christian and Jewish settings at the time). In the prevailing patriarchal ethos, being a man meant protecting the tribe's honour, often entering into feuds with those who had done wrong. Justice was meted out not by judges, but by tribal retribution. It was an age of the blood vendetta, familiar in modern times to those who know *The Godfather* trilogy of films.

Pre-Islamic Arabia was also fairly isolated from the empires on its borders, being surrounded with water on three sides and desert to the north. The Byzantine Empire lay to the west, while the Sassanian Persian Empire was on the east. Both of these empires had battled each other, and were in decline by the time of Muhammad's birth.

When Muhammad began to preach, his message was not well received. This is not surprising, since he was challenging the society of his time. In a time of polytheism, he was preaching monotheism. In a world of drastic social inequality, he was preaching that everyone was equal before God, and that all people were slaves to God. In many ways, his message was similar to the one that Jesus preached some 600 years earlier in Palestine, and like Jesus' followers, Muhammad's disciples were persecuted. Bilal, the Ethiopian slave who later became a religious leader in Medina, was tortured by his owner for converting to Islam. Muhammad sent some of his most vulnerable followers to Ethiopia, where they were protected from persecution by Christians. The persecutions increased after the death of Abu Talib, who had provided his protection to Muhammad. Soon Muhammad and his followers were forced to migrate to Medina, leaving most of their property behind in Mecca.

Permission to fight. In Medina, Muhammad brought unity to the two rival Arab tribes and their Jewish allies who were all trying to control the city. In the Constitution of Medina, Muslims, the polytheistic Arabs, and the Jews were referred to as a single community (*ummah*). Here we see the interactions of religion and politics in early Islam. While the polytheistic Arabs and the Jews accepted Muhammad as their political leader, they were not required to embrace Islam, but they did have to obey Muhammad's political judgments. For the Muslim community, Muhammad was both a religious and political figure, a prophet and a statesman. It was in this context that the first revelations allowing for war were sent down.

To this point, there was no sanction in the Qur'an for any kind of violent response to the persecution that the Muslims had endured. Then came the following verses of the Qur'an: "Permission is given to fight to those upon whom war is made, who were wronged. Truly God is well able to help them, those who were driven out of their homes unjustly, simply because they said our Lord is God. Did not God use some people to repel others, or else monasteries and churches and synagogues and mosques where the name of God is constantly mentioned would have been pulled down? Truly God will help those who help God. Surely God is Almighty" (22:39–40).

The Battle of Badr. Muhammad and his followers felt justified, therefore, in raiding Meccan caravans that were selling goods that the Muslims had left behind during their emigration. In 624, the Meccans learned that Muhammad was going to raid one of their caravans at a watering station named Badr. The Meccans sent their army to that spot, and it was here that the first battle was fought. The Muslims were outnumbered, but were able to defeat the Meccans. In the Muslim understanding, they were victorious because God had helped them (Qur'an 8:17). Later verses also spoke of the battle: "God had helped you at Badr, when you were a contemptible little band. So observe your duties toward God, and thereby show your gratitude. Remember when you [Muhammad] said to the believers: 'Is it not enough that your Lord helped you with 3,000 angels sent down? If you remain steadfast and act aright, even if the enemy should come rushing headlong, your Lord would help you with 5,000 attacking angels'" (Qur'an 3:123–125).

At the Battle of Badr, Muhammad took a number of Meccan captives. The fact that he did not kill his prisoners was out of character in the culture, and is thus instructive for Muslim attitudes to war and vengeance. "Oh Prophet!" says the Qur'an in another revelation about the battle, "Say to those of the captives who are in your hands: If God knows anything good in your hearts, God will give to you better than that which has been taken away from you and will forgive you, and God is Forgiving, Merciful" (8:70).

Chapter Eight of the Qur'an (The Spoils of War) was revealed after the Battle of Badr, and makes further points about how the Muslims should fight against the polytheists of Mecca. It opens with the line that the spoils of war belong to God and God's Messenger. The implication is clear: One does not fight war for gain, since the rewards belong to God. The chapter also states clearly that while Muslims should perpare for war, the Muslims should also prepare for peace with the Meccans: "And if they incline to peace, then incline to it and trust in God; surely God is the Hearing, the Knowing" (8:61).

The Battle of Uhud. The Meccans achieved their revenge a year after the Battle of Badr, when they launched the Battle of Uhud (a hill not far from Medina). Among the Muslim casualties were Muhammad's beloved uncle Hamzah, and Muhammad himself was injured in the fighting. It was in the wake of this battle that Muhammad was forced to deal with one of the Jewish groups in Medina. According to tradition, one of the Jewish clans, sensing the weakness of the Muslims after the defeat at Uhud, attempted to kill the Prophet. As a result, this clan was banished from Medina. A similar situation had taken place following the Battle of Badr, when a different Jewish clan was accused of breaking a pact with the Muslims.

The Battle of the Trench. Two years after their victory at Uhud, the Meccans sought to complete their triumph by completely destroying the Muslims. In 627, they marched on Medina, joined by some of the Jews whom Muhammad had exiled. On the advice of a Muslim supporter, Salman the Persian, the Medinans created a trench around their city. As a result, the Meccan cavalry could not advance into Medina. The Meccans laid siege to the city, but ultimately they could gain no victory. The confederation that the Meccans had created began to break down, and they had to give up the siege and return to Mecca.

During the siege, another of the Jewish groups in Medina was accused of breaking their treaty with Muhammad and aiding the Meccans. As a result, the men of that tribe were ordered to be executed on the judgment of one of the Arab tribes in Medina. Muslims dispute whether this killing actually took place. However, it is clear that Jews who might have been killed in the wake of these battles were executed for treachery and treason, for breaking their treaty with Muhammad, and for working toward the destruction of the Muslim community. They were not executed because they were Jews.

The conquest of Mecca. Muhammad negotiated a peace treaty with the Meccans in 628. This was designed to last for a period of 10 years, but was violated by one of the allies of the Meccans after only two years. As a result, Muhammad and his forces marched on Mecca in 630 and entered the city in triumph, but largely without violence. Muhammad ordered that his army give sanctuary to those who sought it, and to fight only those who fought against them. According to Muslim tradition, only four opponents were killed because of their enmity towards Muhammad. While some may think of this number as four too many, this conquest clearly did not involve the tremendous casualties that warfare in Arabia normally entailed.

Having taken Mecca, Muhammad did something radical. He gathered the leaders of Mecca who had driven him out of the city of his birth and waged war against him for the past five years, and offered them amnesty. By tribal custom, he had every right to execute them, but he chose not to do so. Here Muhammad showed the magnanimity for which he is famous in the Muslim tradition. In freeing his persecutors, he quoted from the words that the Qur'an has Joseph (the son of Jacob) speak when he is reunited with the brothers who sold him into slavery: "This day there shall be no upbraiding of you nor reproach. God forgives you, and God is the Most Merciful of those who show mercy" (12:92). As a result of this generosity, even more people converted to Islam.

In forgiving the Meccans, Muhammad did one of the hardest things for humans: he forgave his enemies. Love for enemies had long been the teaching of Jesus, but as many Christians admit, the fulfillment of the teaching is nearly impossible and is rarely seen to be practical in situations of military conflict. But for Muhammad, forgiveness was the only way forward, and the only way to break the cycle of vengeance and retribution.

The Verse of the Sword. Following the conquest of Mecca, Muslims believe, Chapter Nine of the Qur'an was revealed. This chapter marked the final break between Muhammad and the polytheists of Arabia. This chapter is unusual in being the only one that does not begin with the standard opening, "In the name of God, the Beneficent, the Merciful." The chapter is entitled the "Chapter of Repentance," and the fifth verse of this chapter is known as the Verse of the Sword. It is often quoted by anti-Muslim polemicists, but not usually in its entirety. Verses five and six read:

So when the sacred months have passed away, then slay the polytheists wherever you find them, and take them captive and besiege them and lie in wait for them in every ambush of war, but if they repent and keep up prayer and contribute to charity, leave their way free to them; surely God is Forgiving, Merciful. If any one of the polytheists ask you for asylum, grant it to them, so that they may hear the word of God; and then escort them to a place of safety. That is because they are a people who do not know (9:5–6).

Clearly, this part of the Qur'an sanctions killing. However, it is limited to polytheists, and then only to those who do not denounce their polytheism. In this respect, one could compare the Muslim campaign against polytheists in Arabia to Israel's conquest of pagan peoples in Canaan in the biblical book of Joshua. While there is violence in the Qur'an, it is not an indiscriminate violence. Moreover, it is a violence that is contextualized, meaning it occurs in the context of warfare between Muslims and polytheists. Finally, it is a violence that is tempered, as the following verse indicates: "Fight in the cause of God those who fight you, but do not transgress limits. Surely God does not love the transgressors" (2:190).

The spread and historical development of Islam

In the last two years of Muhammad's life, a number of tribes converted from polytheism to Islam. This may have been due to a number of reasons: a fear of being killed if they didn't convert; an acceptance of Muhammad's message; the personal charisma of the Prophet himself; or a desire to be included in the Muslim community. This last point is particularly important. At the time of Muhammad's death, he was not simply a religious leader, but a political figure as well. Much of the Arabian peninsula had converted to Islam by this time, so Muhammad's political power encompassed an entire region. The early history of Christianity, by contrast, saw the political and the religious spheres united more than three centuries after Jesus, as the Armenians, then the Ethiopians, and finally the Romans adopted Christianity as a state religion. It is for this reason that there is relatively little violence and warfare in the New Testament; the development of principles for a "just war" coincided with the development of a state church. Moreover, unlike Islam, Christianity has free-church streams that regard the shift to an imperial Christianity as a corruption of the ideals of the earliest followers of Jesus. Muslims regard the convergence of religious and political power as a good thing.

There is a popular misconception that Islam was spread primarily by the sword with forced conversions. The historical record does not bear this out. While there certainly were forced conversions in the history of Islam, the great majority of people converted because of their own choice. Take for example the Persian kingdom, which was one of the first to be conquered by the early Muslims. According to historian Richard Bulliet of Columbia University, the conversions in that region happened over many generations. The state religion in Persia before Islam was Zoroastrianism. From the detailed tax records of the Sassanian Empire, one can trace how the Zoroastrian surnames gave way to Muslim ones over time. Thus, over a period of almost 200 years, Persia evolved from a country with no Muslims to a country that was more than 80 percent Muslim. This is a far cry from the image of Arabs on horseback with swords in hand telling people to "convert or die."

Some of the primary agents of conversion were the Sufi mystics, who will be discussed in Chapter Eight. Living among the non-Muslim population, their example and teaching would slowly attract people into Islam. Muslim traders would also help in the spread of Islam, particularly in south and southeast Asia. In many ways, this is no different from the less invasive ways that Christian missionaries have spread Christianity. It is also worth remembering that after the Babylonian Exile (that is, after the sixth century BCE) Judaism encouraged the conversion of non-Jews; the biblical books of Ruth and Jonah, in particular, seem to reflect such a vision of inclusion of non-Jewish people in God's salvation plan. Later, with the development of Christianity, Jewish proselytizers also sought to force Gentile Christians to become Jews.

It is true that Islam expanded rapidly, due to the success of the message preached, the superiority of Muslim military leaders and their tactics, and the historical weakness of both the Byzantine and Persian kingdoms. Over time, people under Muslim rulers gradually converted to Islam. Often, economic factors played a role in the conversion. Christian, Jewish, and Zoroastrians subjects did not have to convert to Islam, since they were considered "People of the Book." They did not have to pay the zakat, the charity incumbent upon all Muslims, and they did not have to serve in the army. However, they were required to pay a special tax in recognition of their non-Muslim status.

While this tax was indeed unfair, history offers many examples of people who are treated differently because they are not considered full citizens of that country. As a Canadian living legally in the United States, for example, I am referred to as a "resident alien." This means that I pay all the taxes that

American citizens pay, including sales tax, state and federal income tax, social security tax, and medicare tax. However, as a non-citizen, I am not eligible to vote in any election, or to serve on a jury. Clearly, there is a difference between my own situation as one who willingly emigrated to another country knowing the rules involved, and the situations of non-Muslim natives of a country taken over by Muslim rulers. The point is that some people converted to Islam to avoid paying the special tax on non-Muslims, indicating that economic reasons sometimes are a factor in decisions about religion.

Islam in the Holy Land. In 638, Muslims conquered Jerusalem under the second Caliph, Umar. According to Muslim tradition, Umar entered Jerusalem on foot because he and his servant shared a single mount, and it was his servant's turn to ride. This gives one an idea of the humanity and humility of Umar. The conquest involved no bloodshed, and all of the inhabitants who wanted to leave were allowed to do so without incident. Umar was escorted around the city by the Greek Orthodox Patriarch. When it came time for one of the daily prayers, Umar was in the Church of the Holy Sepulchre, one of the most important Christian sites in Jerusalem. When he asked for a place to say his prayers, the Patriarch told him to pray where he stood. Umar refused, saying that his later followers, in their zeal, would want to commemorate the spot where Muslims first offered prayer in Jerusalem. This would mean converting the church into a mosque, and this was not something Umar was willing to do. Instead, he prayed outside the church. Sure enough, that spot was eventually marked with the Mosque of Umar. Umar's actions show a wonderful spirit of interfaith dialogue and co-operation. To this day, in fact, the keys to the church gate are kept by a Muslim family, so that various Christian groups don't have to struggle with each other for that honour.

The Crusades and their aftermath. For the most part, Christians were allowed to practice their faith in Jerusalem, unhindered by Muslims. Sadly, the Caliph Al-Hakim destroyed the Church of the Holy Sepulchre in 1009, but he suffered from mental illness and persecuted Muslims as well as Jews and Christians. The church was rebuilt by the Byzantine emperor in 1048. In 1095, Pope Urban the Second called for a Crusade to regain Christian control of the Holy Land. His rationale was religious – that Muslims were not allowing Christians to worship freely. However, this was not entirely the case. There were also underlying economic causes, including a rising class of landless knights in Europe who were increasingly restless and poor. In Palestine, they could either acquire their own land or be killed trying, thereby eliminating them as a threat to the aristocracy of Europe. It is a fascinating exercise to read Muslim accounts of the Crusades, which reveal the economic and religious motivations of the Crusaders. A fascinating study of how the Crusades affected the ways in which Muslims and Christians subsequently understood each other is Norman Daniel's magnificent book *Islam and the West: The Making of an Image* (see "Suggestions for Further Reading" on page 218).

After the Crusades, the Ottoman Turks became the great rival for European Christians. The Ottomans adopted the crescent as their symbol in opposition to the Christian cross, and the crescent has remained as an important Muslim symbol. (The Red Cross, for example, is known as the Red Crescent in the Muslim world, and the crescent adorns the flags of Turkey, Pakistan, Algeria, and Tunisia). The Ottoman Empire was in power as Europe began to regain its supremacy, with European expansionism beginning in the sixteenth century with the "discovery" of America.

By the 19th century, most of the Muslim world was under the colonial domination of Europeans. This colonialism was sometimes described as the "white man's burden" (after Rudyard Kipling's poem on the occasion of the American conquest of the Philippines), or what the French called the *mission civilisatrice* (civilizing mission). As Robert D. Lee wrote in *Rethinking Islam*:

> The periphery became the centre, and the Islamic world found itself marginalised by European imperialism and universalism. Imperialism brought British and French troops, administrators, and merchants to the Middle East and imposed varying degrees of political, economic, and social subordination on the area. That process reached an apogee at Versailles after World War I, when the victors took it upon themselves to dismantle the defeated Ottoman Empire and establish a system of mandates for the governance of the Middle East. No Middle Easterner participated in the decisions.

Much of today's violence in the Muslim world is rooted in the European colonial heritage. This does not excuse the violence; it simply situates the violence in its historical context.

"Democracy" in the Muslim world: Iran and Afghanistan

Recently, especially with the occupation of Iraq, many in the West have been talking about bringing democracy to the Muslim world. Seldom discussed is the fact that many Muslim countries resist democracy precisely because of their experience of European and American colonialism. Such resistance is thoroughly explored in books such as John Esposito's *The Islamic Threat: Myth or Reality?* (see "Suggestions for Further Reading" on page 218). For our purposes here, however, I would like to comment specifically on Iran and Afghanistan at the end of the twentieth century. In what follows, I do not want to be perceived as anti-American. For the past nine years, I have chosen to live in Southern California. Because of my experience in the large, multicultural centres of Toronto, Vancouver, and Montreal, I feel at home in Los Angeles. As a Canadian, I understand how every nation wants to further its own best interests when it relates to the rest of the world. I have observed, however, that the American government has worked against the establishment of democratic reforms when they threaten American interests. In the twentieth century, this has happened in a number of settings, including Guatemala, Brazil, Chile, and Haiti. It has also happened in the Muslim world, ultimately feeding the kind of violence we are seeing today.

The Islamic revolution in Iran. In 1953, the Shah of Iran was overthrown, and a Nationalist government was established by Prime Minister Mohammad Mossadegh. This was to be an Iranian Republic, different from the military dictatorship of the Shah. Before long, however, the CIA helped to engineer the Shah's return to Iran and to re-establish him in power. In return, the Shah allowed American and British firms to run – and profit from – the Iranian oil industry. The United States supported the Shah militarily and helped to train the Shah's secret police. Since Iranian democracy was not in the perceived best interests of the American government in 1953, they did not support it.

As opposition grew to the Shah's regime, one of the few places available to meet and discuss political issues was the mosque. The Shah could shut down the bazaar where people gathered, fearing they might conspire to overthrow him. However, he could not shut down the mosques. In the years leading up to the 1979 revolution under Ayatollah Khomeini, a movement took shape that brought religious fervour together with a renewed desire for political change. Author Salman Rushdie himself, no fan of the Islamic Republic that Iran became, wrote in 1984 that: "We may not approve of Khomeini's Iran, but the revolution there was a genuine mass movement."

The Shah fled Iran in 1979, leaving power to Khomeini, who had been exiled over a decade earlier for his opposition both to the Shah and to the United States. Khomeini, a religious scholar, led the Shi'a clergy in giving shape to the revolution, establishing what would become a theocracy under shari'ah law. It was not surprising that the revolution was followed by a bitter war with Iraq that lasted for eight years. This war was not between religious factions, since both Iraq and Iran had Shi'a majority populations. Instead, it was a clash of dictatorships: Saddam Hussein's military dictatorship in Iraq, versus Khomeini's theocratic dictatorship in Iran. Both wanted to preserve their own rule, as well as control the territory and resources – both human and economic – of the other.

The Iranian revolution was crucial, however, to the aims of Muslim radicals the world over. It showed them that they could defeat a dictator, even one supported by the West, and that it was possible to establish an Islamic regime. This new confidence inspired other acts of violence in the name of religion. In November of 1979, Sunnis seized control of the Grand Mosque in Mecca for two weeks. Subsequently the Shi'as, who make up the majority in Arabia's Eastern Provinces, rioted against the Saudi government, which was Sunni. Both of these uprisings were quelled by the Saudis, but they signalled a willingness among Muslims to fight for what they thought was correct.

The Soviet Invasion of Afghanistan. 1979 was also the year of the Soviet invasion of Afghanistan. In December of that year, the Soviet Army assassinated President Hafizullah Amin and installed another president. The result was a decade-long war against the Soviets. Since this took place during the Cold War, the United States and its allies helped to fund and train the Afghan resistance, the mujahideen. As documented in Mahmood Mamdani's book *Good Muslim, Bad Muslim: America, the Cold War, and the Roots of Terror*, the US Central Intelligence Agency was again instrumental in this intervention; the conflict was one of the largest and most expensive in the history of the CIA.

In some ways, one can regard this invasion as the beginning of a global movement for Muslim violence. Muslims were recruited from all over the world to fight the Soviets. Amazingly, they were able to defeat them. During this time, they were not seen as terrorists, but as freedom fighters, a portrayal that is supported by the movie *Rambo III*, in which a Green Beret goes to Afghanistan to help train the resistance after the Soviets capture his beloved mentor. Having armed the Afghanis in their ousting of the Soviets, Americans were surprised to see these mujahideen turning their guns on each other in a brutal civil war, and then eventually on the United States after the Taliban government came to power.

Another surprise, seldom discussed today, is that in May of 2001, four months before 9-11, the American government gave US $43 million to the Taliban for their help in the war on drugs.

The aid was given in full knowledge that Osama bin Laden was active in anti-American terrorist camps in Afghanistan, and in the face of the Taliban's terrible record on human rights and the treatment of women. The American government's rationale for this grant was the Taliban's claim that the growing of opium was un-Islamic. I shudder to think what the Taliban did with that money!

The complexities of "Muslim violence"

It surprises many North Americans that most Muslims are opposed to violence and terrorism. Like all people, Muslims want to live in peace and safety. That this has to be made explicit indicates the sorry state of understanding between Muslims and non-Muslims. I cannot remember the last time I gave a talk to a non-Muslim group in the past five years where someone didn't ask me if I was opposed to terrorism. I am reminded of a story by the American folk singer Arlo Guthrie. Knowing his work for social justice, someone asked him to join a group of artists and musicians against hunger, to which Guthrie replied incredulously, "You mean there are artists and musicians *for* hunger?"

A few Muslims are actively involved in peace and justice groups. One such group, the Muslim Peace Fellowship, has existed for more than a decade in the United States, and is affiliated with the Fellowship of Reconciliation. These groups have strenuously worked to contradict the claim, often repeated in the American media since 9-11, that Muslims have not condemned terrorism. One still encounters this disturbing perception repeatedly – in letters to the editor in local American newspapers, as well as in right-wing websites that are easily found on the Internet. But the record is clear: Hours after the horrors of 9-11, the Muslim Public Affairs Council, the Council on American Islamic Relations, and the American Muslim Political Coordination Council all issued statements condemning the attacks and offering their resources to help the victims. On the following Friday, September 14, Muslim leaders around the world condemned the attacks in their Friday sermons. Shaykh Al-Tantawi of Egypt's Al-Azhar University, one of the most respected Sunni institutions, declared: "It is not courageous to attack innocent children, women and civilians. It is courageous to protect freedom, it is courageous to defend oneself and not to attack." Significantly, both Iranian President Mohammed Khatami and Shaykh Fadlallah, the spiritual leader of Hizbullah, said that the attacks were barbaric and un-Islamic.

Suicide bombings. Another common misconception is that Muslims value suicide bombing. As with other religious traditions, suicide is explicitly forbidden in Islam. It is seen as challenging the authority of God who determines the span of our lives. So, for example, the Qur'an states: "Do not kill yourselves, truly God is Merciful to you" (4:29). It is true that the Qur'an promises a heavenly reward to those who die in defence of the faith, but suicide is not part of that vision:

> Oh you who believe! Be not like those who disbelieve and say of their brethren when they travel in the earth or engage in fighting: Had they been with us, they would not have died and they would not have been slain; so God makes this to be an intense regret in their hearts; and God gives life and causes death and God sees what you do. And if you are slain in the way of God or you die, certainly forgiveness from God and mercy is better than what they amass. And if indeed you die or you are

slain, certainly to God you will be gathered together (3:156–158).

Also contrary to popular belief, the Qur'an never specifies that martyrs will receive a certain number of virgins as part of their reward.

So why do some Muslims conduct suicide bombings in the name of their faith? If one looks beneath the surface, one often discovers economic and political motivations rather than religious ones. The case of the Israeli/Palestinian conflict makes this clear. Palestinian terrorists do not attack Israelis because they are Jews but because of the political and economic ramifications of the Israeli occupation of Palestine. It is also understandable that a young Palestinian man who has no hope for a reasonable future in the Occupied Territories, would volunteer to blow himself up if his family would receive financial support from a sponsoring organization.

Another bit of information that people in the West tend to forget is that suicide bombing is not only a Muslim phenomenon. In fact, Robert Pape, in his brilliant book *Dying to Win: The Strategic Logic of Suicide Terrorism*, indicates that that from 1980 to 2004 the world leader in suicide terrorism was not a Muslim group, but the Tamil Tigers (a Marxist Hindu group) in Sri Lanka.

The duplicity of our governments: state terrorism

As we examine the actions of individual terrorists, we cannot hide from a larger reality that often provides context for such acts: the violence and terror perpetrated by states. To return to the Israeli/Palestinian scene, when a Palestinian civilian kills an Israeli soldier, our media call it an act of terrorism. However, when an Israeli soldier kills a Palestinian civilian, that is usually termed a security operation, not an act of terrorism. Again, let me be very clear: I condemn all terrorism and violence. I have been in a café in Jerusalem, afraid that I might be killed by a Palestinian suicide bomber. But in Israel I have also been afraid of being killed in a military operation, or shot by an Israeli settler. Neither of those options, of course, is acceptable to me.

But when I raise the larger issues among audiences who are both pro-Zionist and anti-Palestinian, I am often accused of being unhelpful. Many people find it difficult to examine complex roots of a problem; it is much simpler to treat the immediate symptoms. The late Brazilian Archbishop Dom Helder Camara once said: "When I give food to the poor, they call me a saint. When I ask why the poor have no food, they call me a communist." To apply that complaint to the terrorism discussion, some people rightly want to condemn terrorism, but don't want to ask the deeper questions of why people resort to terrorism. But we must address the deeper questions if we want to put an end to terrorism.

In the Israeli/Palestinian discussions, therefore, let us certainly bring to the table the violence of suicide bombers and other terrorists. But let us also bring larger inequities and prejudices, such as the following: (1) The automatic entitlement to Israeli citizenship based on religious identity. While there are Arabs (both Christian and Muslim) who have Israeli citizenship, they are a minority and they do not have rights equal to Jewish Israelis. (2) The extent of casualties. By conservative estimates, Israelis have killed three times more Palestinians than Palestinians have killed Israelis. (3) Simplistic understandings of complex communities. Although 15 percent of the Palestinians are Christians with very deep historical roots,

North Americans think of them almost entirely as Muslims. We think of Palestinian actions as being rooted in their Muslim faith. Ironically, we do not think of the actions of the Israeli Defence Forces – Jewish soldiers defending a Jewish state – as being Jewish.

When the state kills in our name, we tend not to think of that as violence. By the end of 2001, some three months after the war in Afghanistan began, United States Armed Forces with the help of coalition forces (including Canadian soldiers) had killed more than 3,000 Afghanis in our war with them. In number, this was approximately equal to the number killed in the terrorist attacks of 9-11. Even more disturbing is that by conservative estimates, some 20,000 Iraqis had been killed by the third anniversary of the invasion of Iraq, almost seven times the number who perished in 9-11. All this took place ostensibly as part of the "war on terrorism" even though there was never any demonstrated link between Saddam Hussein's dictatorship in Iraq and the terrorist attacks of 9-11. By comparing the numbers of victims, I am not advocating any calculus of suffering. The loss of one person is already a tragedy. Yet the losses among our enemies usually do not figure in our thinking.

Our own violence

Just as we are blind to the violence of our governments, we also tend to ignore the violence in our own culture and in our own lives. We may not think much about the history of violence in North America, particularly the violent impact of European colonialism on the indigenous peoples of the Americas. Christians may similarly forget or downplay the Christian affiliations and commitments of the Nazis, whose religion failed to stop them from carrying out the Holocaust. Or we may think we abhor violence, yet blithely glorify it in hymns like "The Battle Hymn of the Republic" (one of the hymns that was sung at the first United Methodist church service I ever attended).

We may not think of the violence that is all around us. In contemporary America, some 10,000 people are murdered annually by handguns; almost the same number die in handgun suicides. Since the reinstatement of the death penalty in the United States in 1976, over 1,000 people have been executed by the state. One of the most serious issues faced by young people in our cities is gang life. Our movies, television shows, video games, and music all celebrate a culture of violence. In 2006, the Academy Award for best original song went to "It's hard out here for a pimp," which glorifies the sexual and economic exploitation of women.

Violence is therefore integrated into the very structure of our society. We live in a complex web in which the violence "out there" is connected to our own violence in more ways than we may acknowledge. It is tempting to project our own violence to someone else, preferably someone – a nation, an ethnic group, or a religion – that is markedly different from our own. Without excusing any of the violence committed by Muslims, one can see how it is often connected to economic exploitation, military occupation, or the achievement of political goals. However, it is usually simply labelled as "Muslim" violence, as if religion is the sole motivation for the violence.

It is much simpler to blame 9-11 and other terrorist acts on Muslims in general, rather than on specific Muslims who have departed from their own religious ideals. Even to acknowledge that not all Muslims are terrorists, however, does not get at the root of the problem. While it takes a great deal of analysis, humility, and courage, the kind of acknowledgement we all need these days is that we and our society are, to a great extent, enmeshed in, and part of the violence we decry. Insomuch as that enmeshment is between Muslims and Christians, that is the very reason why we need to learn to dialogue more deeply together.

7

Roles of women and men

In 2000, two different advertising campaigns in Los Angeles featured images of veiled women. The first was for the opening of the renovated Aladdin Hotel and Casino in Las Vegas, a day's drive across the desert. Billboards featured the head and shoulders of an attractive Middle Eastern woman with an enticing smile, wearing a delicate veil that covered her hair and lower face. It was a classic image of the "erotic Orient" – a harem girl available for one's sexual pleasure. Clearly, the casino saw this image as one that would attract gambling tourists to Las Vegas.

The other campaign was for the *Los Angeles Times*, one of the most respected newspapers in America. The campaign, entitled "Connecting us to the Times," included television commercials, print ads, billboards, and bus ads. In each advertisement, an image of bikini-clad women on a Southern California beach was juxtaposed with an image of women wearing full black Afghani *burqas*, the robes that cover women from head to toe. In many ways, this ad was more troubling than the first one. While one expects Las Vegas casinos to use sex to sell its products, why would a non-tabloid newspaper do the same thing? In this case, the veiled women suggested suppressed sexuality, only highlighting the overt sexuality of the women in bikinis. The ads were criticized by Muslim groups, but also by 200 *Times* employees who objected to the use of women's bodies – covered or uncovered – to sell their product. As a result, the *Times* cancelled the campaign.

These two campaigns in North America showed distorted images of Muslim women around the world. In the Victorian era, English colonists criticized Muslims for being too sensual. In this modern age of sexual liberation, the veiled Muslim woman represents a repressed or oppressed sexuality. Both images are full of prejudice and misunderstanding regarding the roles of women in Islam and in Muslim society. This chapter seeks to work towards a greater appreciation for gender issues in Islam. It is important to set that discussion properly in the context of history. I begin, therefore, with a brief survey of pre-Islamic customs, and of how shari'ah law (see Chapter Five) was a response to them. I then move to a more specific discussion on how the law affects women, particularly with respect to the issues of veiling, marriage, polygamy, and male authority over women. I end with contemporary issues of women leading prayer and the 2005 debate in Ontario about a bid to introduce shari'ah law in North America.

Pre-Islamic and Islamic understandings of the position of women

In Arabia before Islam, women generally filled a very low social position. A woman was treated as property, essentially sold by her father or guardian to her husband, who was then free to do with her as he wanted. A man could marry an unlimited number of wives, divorce them at will, and not be required to pay them any support. Female infanticide was practiced in pre-Islamic Arabia, since sons were considered more valuable than daughters.

It was into this world that Muhammad came with a divine message of social justice. First, the Qur'an forbade the killing of infant girls, and declared that daughters were as highly valued as sons (16:57–59 and 81:8–9). Muhammad's own example supported the Qur'an's teaching; he and Khadija had four daughters whom they loved very much, and no sons who survived past infancy. Second, as discussed below, Islamic law placed limits on marriage and divorce, and allowed women the right to sue for divorce on certain grounds. Third, the Islamic legal tradition instituted a dowry for women, which would serve as support in case of divorce.

The position of women under Islamic law, therefore, was much better than their position in pre-Islamic Arabia. Admittedly, there have been a great many advantages that women in the West have gained in the past two centuries, giving them more rights than women who live under Islamic law. For many progressive Muslims, however, the issue is not Islamic law itself, but the legal traditions that have been created, argued, and interpreted largely by men. Historically, there have been female jurists, including 2003 Nobel Peace Prize winner, Shirin Ebadi of Iran. But they have been small in number when compared with men. In the modern world, Muslim women and men are challenging some of the legal rulings that may have been helpful in an earlier time, but are harmful in today's world.[1]

Islamic law and women

When discussing the roles and lives of Muslim women today, it is important at the outset to avoid making generalizations and to remember the particular contexts of individual women. A snapshot of the varied and contradictory contexts of women in North America can help us understand why: Being a woman in Los Angeles, for example, is a very different experience for a wealthy and famous movie star than it is for a homeless woman living with her children on skid row. Or look at the roles of women in political life. Both in Canada and the United States, women are theoretically equal to men, yet neither country has elected a female head of state. (Kim Campbell's short stint as prime minister in the 1980s was the result of the mid-term resignation of Brian Mulroney, not a national election.) By contrast, Pakistan, Bangladesh, and Turkey – all with predominantly Muslim populations – have elected women as leaders. It is therefore simplistic to hold up North America as being progressive, and the Muslim world as being oppressive in the treatment of women.

Muslims need to remember the example of the Prophet Muhammad in any discussion of the legal roles of men and women. A number of instructive details of his first marriage, to Khadija, show that Muhammad was not bound to the patriarchy of his time. First, she was independently wealthy, and in fact hired Muhammad to sell her goods. Second, she initiated her own marriage by proposing to Muhammad without using a male guardian as an intermediary. Third, she had been previously married and widowed, while Muhammad was unmarried. Fourth, she was older than Muhammad; traditional sources say that she was 40 years old while he was 25. Finally, it was a monogamous marriage. Muhammad would have no other wives while Khadija was alive. For many Muslim women and men, it is Khadija that stands as the example for Muslim women, and they demand nothing more – or less – than the rights that she had.

Unfortunately, many Muslims are not aware of these details. Religious illiteracy is as prevalent in the Muslim world as it is among Christians. Moreover, religious leaders who would oppress women deliberately keep this information about the Prophet from them. As noted earlier, the interpreters of the early example of Muhammad were mostly male. The Islamic legal and religious traditions have been almost exclusively interpreted by men. As a result many Muslim women are unaware of their own tradition. By contrast, Muslim feminists, who have studied the life of Muhammad, look to the Prophet as a man who enjoyed the company of women, who spoke with them, taught them, learned from them, and took them seriously. As will be discussed later, there is a new generation of Muslim women scholars who are reinterpreting the tradition to reclaim the history of the Prophet, and a new generation of Muslim women who are demanding the rights due to them as women.

Seclusion and veiling

In much of the modern Muslim world, public space has become male space. This is discussed in the work of a Moroccan Muslim feminist, Fatima Mernissi. She decries the situation in her home country, where she cannot take public transportation or wander around the city centre without being harassed by men. Unfortunately, those circumstances are also known to some women in North America. Seclusion of women dates to the time of Muhammad's subsequent marriages following the death of Khadija. The following passage from the Qur'an gives a window into the origins of the practice:

> Oh you who believe! Do not enter not the Prophet's houses – until leave is given you – for a meal, and then not so early as to wait for its preparation... And when

you ask his wives for anything that you want, ask them from in front of a screen [*hijab*]: that makes for greater purity for your hearts and for theirs. Nor is it right for you that you should annoy God's Messenger, or that you should marry his widows after him at any time. Truly such a thing is an enormity in the sight of God. Whether you reveal anything or conceal it, truly God has full knowledge of all things. There is no blame if these women appear before their fathers or their sons, their brothers, or their brothers' sons, or their sisters' sons, or their women, or the slaves whom they own. And women, fear God; for God is witness to all things (33:53–55).

Here we see the use of the term *hijab* to mean a screen or barrier, a curtain to divide the public space from the private space in the houses of the wives of the Prophet. In this text, the *hijab* applied only to interactions with the wives of the Prophet, known to Muslims by their honorific title, "The Mothers of the Believers." The wives of the Prophet were free to appear in front of family members or servants without being hidden, but for visitors were required to be secluded.

    Another verse speaks of all women having to cover themselves: "And those who annoy believing men and women undeservedly, bear the guilt of slander and a glaring sin. Oh Prophet! Tell your wives and daughters, and the believing women, that they should cast their outer garments over their persons. That is most convenient, that they should be recognized and not molested. And God is ever forgiving, most merciful" (33:58–59). Here, all Muslim women are told that they should wear a loose outer garment over their clothes, so that they will be recognized as Muslim women. However, this verse does not mandate any sort of head or face covering for women. Also, note that the first line speaks about the behaviour of people who harass Muslims, whether men or women.

The veil

The Qur'an requires modesty for both men and women:

Say to the believing men that they should lower their gaze and guard their modesty: that will make for greater purity for them. God is well acquainted with all that they do. Say to the believing women that they should lower their gaze and guard their modesty; that they should not display their beauty except what must ordinarily appear; that they should draw their veils over their bosoms and not display their beauty except to their husbands, their fathers, their husband's fathers, their sons, their husband's sons, their brothers or their brothers' sons, or their sisters' sons, or their women, or the slaves whom they own, or male servants free of physical needs, or small children who do not know about the nakedness of women; and that they should not stamp their feet in order to draw attention to their hidden ornaments. Oh believers! Turn you all together towards God, so that you might succeed (24:30–31).

As Muslim women have pointed out, this verse is clear that men and women will encounter each other in the same public space. When they do so, both men and women are given the same instructions: "Lower your gaze and guard your modesty." The Qur'an gives no explicit instructions for what this modest dress is for women, other than saying that they are to draw their veils across their chest, and not put on unnecessary displays. As a result, there are many different interpretations of how Muslim women should dress.

Islamic tradition does require, however, that Muslim women cover their hair when they pray. This is based on an interpretation of the Qur'an passage just quoted, which assumes that the veil covering the bosom is also covering the hair. Some Muslim women cover their hair at all times, while others do so only when in public or at worship. Some Muslim women cover their entire hair and face with a veil. Other Muslim women cover their hair and part of their face. It is clear, therefore, that Muslims have widely differing interpretations of what it means to dress modestly and not to draw attention to one's beauty. These varied veiling practices, interestingly, find parallels within other faith traditions, particularly the Orthodox Jewish or conservative Mennonite communities.

Culture and ethnicity usually determine the kind of dress that may be worn by women. A Muslim businesswoman in India might wear a sari with a veil around her head and shoulders, but when she travels to North America, she might wear something different. The rule, however, is that the dress be modest. Ideally, women should be free to make their own decisions about what constitutes modest dress. In Muslim homes and societies, however, those decisions are often made by the men who have authority over them, or by the state. There may also be particular laws in a country governing how women should dress, and these may change from time to time. For example, the Shah of Iran, in attempting to Westernize the country, made it illegal for women to wear the veil in public. After the 1979 Islamic revolution, the government made it illegal for women *not* to wear the veil in public. To force reluctant women to wear the veil, however, violates the Muslim spirit. All religious practices should be done out of a desire to please God, not humans.

As suggested in the earlier quote from the Qur'an, women are free to dress however they like in private. Even in Iran, where women are punished by religious authorities for appearing in public without appropriate covering, they may (and do) wear the latest in European fashions in the privacy of their homes.

For many Muslim women in North America, wearing the veil is as much a political statement as it is a religious statement. It is a public proclamation of their Muslim identity. With the rise of anti-Muslim sentiment, some Muslim women have taken off their veils, while others have put them on.[2] Similarly, Muslim women who choose to dress conservatively make a statement about contemporary attitudes towards fashion and women's lives. They want to be taken seriously for who they are, and judged by the content of their character and the quality of their thought, not on the appearance of certain physical attributes.

The dress of women, of course, is related to the behaviour of men. The same woman dressed in a short skirt may be harassed by men who would greet her respectfully if she was dressed in a more conservative manner. In some ways, most men can relate to this preferential treatment. I notice the different way I am treated when I walk into a business wearing a coat and tie as opposed to jeans and a t-shirt. My ordained male colleagues at Loyola Marymount University are treated differently when they wear clerical collars than when they wear golf shirts. Islamic approaches to dress for women, however, recognize the cross-gender sexual dynamic that exists between men and women – hence an emphasis on modesty.

Marriage and polygamy

There is a common misconception among many North Americans that most Muslims are polygamous. In fact, the opposite is true; about 95 percent of married Muslims are in monogamous relationships. However, polygamy is permitted within the Islamic legal tradition. Admittedly, Islam does include gender inequality in that a man may marry up to four wives, but a woman may have only one husband. Also, a Muslim man may marry a Muslim, Jewish, Christian, or Zoroastrian woman in an Islamic marriage, while a Muslim woman is permitted to marry only a Muslim male.

Many of the traditions around Muslim marriage are rooted in Muhammad's own example. After the death of Khadija, the Prophet did marry a number of wives. The usual list of his wives after Khadija includes: Sawda, A'isha, Hafsa, Zaynab bint Khuzayma, Umm Salamah Hind, Zaynab bint Jahsh, Juwayriyya, Safiyya, Ramla, and Maymuna. Most of the women he married were older widows, including Sawda, his first wife after Khadija. Some of the women represented alliances between families; A'isha and Hafsa were the daughters of his companions Abu Bakr and Umar, who would become the first two Caliphs after Muhammad's death.

The ten wives after Khadija are more than the limit of four wives that the Qur'an puts on other men. As a Prophet, therefore, Muhammad was exempt from certain rules required for other people. Unlike other women, his wives were forbidden in the Qur'an to remarry after his death. Also, at one point he was given a slave woman, Marya the Copt, who became his concubine and was later freed. Clearly, Muhammad was attracted to women. For Muslims, this confirms the full humanity of the Prophet; sexual activity was as important to him as it is to anyone else. Yet Islamic law limits sexual activity to heterosexual, marital relationships. There are gay, lesbian, bisexual, and transgendered Muslims who seek equal status, and in North America these have formed groups such as Queer Jihad or the Al-Fatiha Foundation. They argue that their sexuality is God-given and should be honoured by other Muslims. However, they face a great deal of discrimination from much of the Muslim community.

Some non-Muslims are concerned that the Prophet married a young girl, A'isha, even though the marriage was not consummated until after she reached puberty. For Muslims, there is nothing wrong with this marriage, given that it was for the Prophet and happened in a much earlier time. For me, part of Muhammad's attraction to A'isha must have been her youth, but not in the way that most people think an older man is sexually attracted to a younger woman. I see it more in terms of a legacy; A'isha, being much younger than Muhammad, would be able to pass along information about him to later generations. In fact, she did this, and a number of hadiths have A'isha as their source.

Historically, the marriage of young girls to men has occurred in the Muslim world, and unfortunately it still occurs in some parts of the Muslim world today. Many Muslims, however, frown on this practice as both parties in a wedding must be able to give their informed consent. In many parts of the Muslim world, there are minimum ages for people to marry and engage in sexual activity.

The Qur'an does allow for polygamy. However, the context in which it addresses the subject is a concern for social justice and respect for mothers:

Oh humanity! Reverence your Guardian-Lord, who created you from a single person, created of like nature its mate, and from the two scattered countless men and women; reverence God, through whom you demand your mutual rights, and reverence the wombs that bore you, for God ever watches over you. And give to orphans their property, nor substitute your worthless things for their good ones; and devour not their property as an addition to your own. For this is indeed a great sin. If you fear that you shall not be able to deal justly with the orphans, marry women of your choice, two or three or four; but if you fear that you shall not be able to deal justly with them, then only one, or a slave that your right hands possess, that will be more suitable, to prevent you from doing injustice (4:1–3).

This passage begins with reverence for God who creates all life, but also exhorts hearers to reverence the women who gave birth to all of us.[3] It goes on to speak of the mutual rights that men and women are to share, and of the ethical and just treatment of orphans.

The passage also suggests polygamy as an answer to the economic exploitation of women and children. As noted earlier, the injunction on polygamy may have limited the custom in pre-Islamic Arabia that allowed men to have many more than four wives, which seemed to exacerbate the exploitation of women. However, the passage also states that one may marry more than one wife only if one can deal justly with them. This is elaborated later in the same chapter:

They ask your instruction concerning the women. Say: God does instruct you about them: And remember what was recited to you in the Book, concerning the orphans of women to whom you do not give the portions prescribed, and yet whom you desire to marry, as also concerning the children who are weak and oppressed: that you stand firm for justice to orphans. There is not a good deed which you do, but God is well-acquainted with it. If a wife fears cruelty or desertion on her husband's part, there is no blame on them if they arrange an amicable settlement between themselves; and such settlement is best; even though men's souls are swayed by greed. But if you do good and practise self-restraint, God is well-acquainted with all that you do. You are never able to be fair and just as between women, even if it is your ardent desire (4:127–129).

For many Muslims, the statement that "you are never able to be fair and just as between women" makes the condition of polygamy impossible, which may explain that the vast majority of Muslims are in monogamous marriages.

Male authority

Perhaps no verses in the Qur'an are more of an issue for Muslim feminists than the following:

Men are the maintainers of women, because God has made some of them to excel others, and because they support them from their means. Therefore the righteous women are obedient, and guard in secret what God would have them guard. As to those women on whose part you fear disloyalty and ill-conduct, admonish them, then refuse to share their beds, and last beat them lightly; but if they obey you, do not seek a way against them. For

God is great and most high. If you fear a breach between the two, appoint two arbiters, one from his family, and the other from hers; if they wish for peace, God will cause their reconciliation. For God has full knowledge, and is acquainted with all things (4:34–35).

Muslim feminists understand the first part of this passage to be speaking about the economic superiority of men over women – that some men excel over some women because they have more economic power. Under Islamic law, a man is required to provide for his family, but if a woman works, the money is hers to do with as she pleases and she has no obligation to contribute it to the family.

Tragically, some Muslim men have used this verse to justify the abuse of women. They feel that they are superior to women in all ways, and not just in terms of wage-earning. The Qur'an does allow men to beat their wives as a last resort in cases of extreme marital discord. The tradition of the Prophet Muhammad, who never beat any of his wives, is that this should be a symbolic beating. Muslim feminists, of course, have great trouble with any sort of beating, symbolic or otherwise. They interpret this verse to be subservient to the Qur'an's overall emphasis on justice and its stand against oppression. They argue that a marriage should never get to the point of justifying any kind of beating, since the end of this passage also requires arbitration from both sides in the case of serious difficulties.

Equality of men and women

In a number of passages, the Qur'an addresses both men and women, giving them both identical duties and an identical reward. For example:

The believers, men and women, are protectors one of another: they enjoin what is just, and forbid what is evil: they observe regular prayers, practise regular charity, and obey God and God's Messenger. On them will God pour mercy: for God is exalted in power, wise. God has promised to believers, men and women, gardens to live in under which rivers flow, and beautiful mansions in gardens of everlasting bliss. But the greatest bliss is the good pleasure of God: that is the supreme achievement (Qur'an 9:71–72).

From this verse, it is clear that men and women are responsible for taking care of each other, making sure that they do good and refrain from evil. Muslim feminists use verses like this one to contextualize the injunction about beating in 4:34. Clearly, one cannot protect someone if one is beating them, and clearly from this verse women have just as much of a duty to protect men as men do to protect women. Both men and women are commanded to do the same things, and both are promised the same reward. There is no sense that only men are rewarded with heaven, or that women are exempt from everlasting bliss.

Another verse is even more explicit about what can be expected by both men and women:

For Muslim men and women – for believing men and women, for devout men and women, for true men and women, for men and women who are patient and constant, for men and women who humble themselves, for men and women who give in charity, for men and women who fast, for men and women who guard their chastity, and for men and women who engage much in

God's praise – for them has God prepared forgiveness and great reward (33:35).

Muslim feminists place great emphasis on the language of this verse, which speaks to both men and women. Women are addressed as women, and not subsumed as a category of men. Moreover, men and women are given the same injunctions to be patient, to humble themselves, and to guard their chastity. There are no special privileges given to men but denied to women in this verse. Both men and women receive the rewards that result from worshipping God.

Women leading prayer?

In March of 2005, Dr. Amina Wadud led a mixed-gender Muslim prayer service in New York City. The event caused a great deal of controversy, because it broke a number of Islamic conventions. It involved a woman leading a mixed gender group, even though convention says that women can lead prayer only among other women or within their own family. At the service, men and women were beside each other in rows, even though the rules say that the rows must be separated by gender. Finally, some of the women had their hair uncovered, which violates the rule about veiling.

As a Muslim, I would not have participated in the prayer, but neither would I have protested against it. For me, it was not the issue of female leadership. Dr. Wadud, whom I have long admired for her scholarly work on issues of Islam and gender, is much more devout and learned than I am. I would consider it an honour to pray under her leadership. My own personal barrier against participating in the prayer would have been the mixing of men and women in rows. Like many other

Muslims, I think that women should have space beside men for prayer, and not be shunted off to balconies or basements as happens in many mosques. However, because of the physical action involved in prayer, I support the notion of separating the rows by gender. The only time that this interspersing occurs in a way accepted by all Muslims is during the pilgrimage to Mecca, where men and women encircle the Ka'ba and pray beside each other. However, this is considered to be a special practice reserved only for the pilgrimage.

The prayer service in New York may have started a new trend; I know of at least one other service that occurred since, in Toronto. I expect the issue of mixed gender prayers led by women will be an important one for North American Muslims in the years to come, just as expectations and roles around gender have become issues for other faith traditions.

The shari'ah law debate in Ontario: creating and maintaining Muslim identity

In 2005 there was significant discussion in the province of Ontario about the use of faith-based arbitration. Fourteen years earlier, in 1991, the province had allowed for such arbitration to be used among religious groups in settling family disputes. This was not for criminal law, and nothing that an arbitrator decided was allowed to contravene the Criminal Code of Canada. Faith-based arbitration was a way for people who wanted to settle issues such as divorce and inheritance to do this outside of the courts. A few Muslim lawyers had been lobbying since this time to go further and to have shari'ah law recognized as a legitimate form of arbitration for those who sought it.

This case is significant for our discussion, since it illustrates the challenge for Muslims in North America who seek to participate in the society that is now their home – especially in effecting change in the legal system.

The opposition to the bid to include shari'ah law included groups of Muslims who were concerned about the potential for abuse, especially in the treatment of women. There were particular concerns in the rules of inheritance, where women under shari'ah would sometimes be given less of a share than would men. In its origins, this rule was advantageous to women who were not able to inherit any property at all, but in an egalitarian society like Canada's, the rule no longer held any appeal. Proponents countered that men would sometimes need a larger share because they have to support the women in their families, particularly they needed to pay alimony payments over an extended period of time. Interestingly, some Muslim proponents saw this shari'ah arbitration system as a test case for other Muslims to follow in seeking to apply their shari'ah values in a non-Muslim context.

Still, the opposition was strong, and was symbolized in a brochure that was published at the time. An image of a woman from south Asia – her religious identity is unclear – adorned the cover of the brochure, entitled "Behind Closed Doors". The woman on the brochure stood in front of two faceless women who were seated. For me, the subtext was clear: "we" (the women of privilege who produced the brochure) need to protect "them" (poor immigrant Muslim women of colour) from "themselves" (the women themselves, as well as the Muslim men who would exploit them), or else we might see Canada take a step backwards, away from our values of equality. I had observed scenes like this in the 1970s and 1980s when immigrant women of colour in Toronto had to fight for their places among white women's groups. It was disheartening to see it again in the year 2005. It was a reminder that even as we North Americans try to address individual issues of race, class, religion, or gender individually (in this case gender) we still can miss our complicity in other forms of oppression (such as racism).

On the other hand, the content of the brochure pointed in the right direction. It laid out a fearsome scenario of a movement to impose Iran-style law in Ontario, and eventually in other provinces. Like most Ontarians, the brochure opposed any kind of faith-based arbitration, Muslim or otherwise. In the end, the opponents prevailed and the ruling was announced, coincidentally, on September 11, 2005, ending the privileges that were available to some faiths but not others. As a Muslim, I applauded the decision. There should either be faith-based arbitration for all faiths, or the entire system should be abolished.

However, as a Muslim, I was also concerned about much of the anti-Muslim rhetoric expressed in the debate. Especially disturbing was the idea – expressed by both Muslims and non-Muslims – that somehow Muslims were not to be trusted with the power of arbitration. This raises the broader question of whether Muslims, as Muslims, are allowed to work to change their society. When women, people of colour, or gays and lesbians initially began to work for legal change, they encountered similar opposition, but eventually won their rights. Perhaps there will be a similar future for North American Muslims, where instead of only being changed by their society, they in turn are able to change it.

8

Sufism:
a romance with God

North Americans today are more and more interested in the mystical traditions of the world's religions. In Los Angeles and New York celebrities seem to be leading the way. Madonna and Britney Spears are learning about Kabbalah, a mystical stream within Judaism, while Richard Gere and Steven Segal have passed along Tibetan Buddhist teachings of the Dalai Lama. For decades, Leonard Cohen has promoted the Zen form of Buddhism. In a materialistic culture like ours, alternative teachings that speak to our spirits have keen appeal. We know deep down the truth of the old Catholic saying, "You don't have a soul, you *are* a soul. You have a body."

It is not surprising, therefore, that at the end of the twentieth century, the best-selling poet in America was a thirteenth century mystic. But not everyone knows that this poet, Jalal al-Din Rumi, was also Muslim. Rumi wrote poetry in Persian and Arabic from the Muslim spiritual tradition known as Sufism. Rumi's poetry reflects a deep yearning for

God – a pull that is felt by all those who long for God, whether they are Jewish, Christian, or Muslim, or belong to any other monotheistic tradition. One of Rumi's most famous lines is: "There are many ways to kneel and kiss the ground." This refers to the specific Muslim practice of prayer, but it resonates with all of those who bow down to God in their own ways. The union with God that the mystic seeks transcends gender, ethnicity, ego, or even religious tradition – those things that often cause divisions and strife among humans. A discussion of Sufism, therefore, is indispensable when one explores interfaith relationships between Muslims and Christians.

What is Sufism and who is a Sufi?

The name *Sufism* comes from the Arabic word *tasawwuf,* or "the process of becoming a Sufi." Sufism is experiential in nature, involving a commitment to personal transformation. The root meaning of *Sufi* is "wool," which is consistent with the ascetic character of the beginnings of Sufism. Early followers would wear woollen garments in conscious opposition to the wearing of more expensive fabrics such as silk and satin. They were reacting to the worldliness that came with the expansion of Islamic civilization in the eighth century. In time, however, the asceticism gave way to a tradition that included the appreciation of the arts, including exquisite, sensual poetry.

Sufism cuts across divisions within Islam, just as Christian mysticism often cuts through denominational barriers. Sufis are male and female, and they include Sunni and Shi'a Muslims. They are organized in many communities or orders throughout the world. Just as there are a great many ways to be Muslim, so there are a great many ways to be a Sufi Muslim. Some Sufis show what may appear to be an anti-intellectualism in their pursuit of direct experiences of the divine. Some speak of their mystical understandings in the language of complex philosophy. Others emphasize ritual practices such as turning in circles or singing devotional songs.

Muhammad as model Sufi

Sufism is deeply rooted in the Qur'an and in the example of the Prophet Muhammad. As Muslims, Sufis believe that the Qur'an is a direct revelation from God to the Prophet Muhammad. Sometimes the revelations came through the angel Gabriel, but at other times Muhammad had mystical experiences that he compared to the ringing of a bell, leaving him shaken. Sufis know that they are not prophets, but they nevertheless understand Muhammad as their model, and aspire to the same direct experience of the divine that Muhammad had.

Apart from the experience of the revelations themselves, Muhammad is also known for his famous ascension into heaven, alluded to in Chapter Three. As the Qur'an describes it: "Glory to God who took God's servant on a night journey from the sacred mosque to the furthest mosque upon which we have sent down our blessing, that we might show him some of our signs. God is the All-Hearing, the All-Seeing" (17:1). This verse has traditionally been interpreted as describing Muhammad's night journey (*mi'raj*) from the Ka'ba in Mecca ("the sacred mosque") to a place in Jerusalem ("the furthest mosque"). From this spot (now housed in the Dome of the Rock), Muhammad ascended through the seven heavens until he was brought into the presence of God. Muslims believe this journey prefigures the time when they will be reunited with God at the Hour of Judgment. Sufis, however, are those Muslims who yearn for that reunion in this life.

One of the most important Sufi practices is known as *dhikr* (remembrance). The Qur'an encourages a constant remembrance of God in a general sense, but Sufis make a devotional practice of it. In meditation, they will often repeat – silently or aloud – the name of God or one or more of God's attributes. Often, they will use a string of beads to count out their repetitions, in much the same way that Catholics pray the rosary or Buddhists use prayer beads.

This meditation is one of the first steps on the journey to union with God. In many ways, it can be compared to the "Jesus prayer" of the Orthodox Christian tradition, where the believer is to utter the name of Jesus with each breath. One does not remember the name of God as an intellectual exercise alone, but may accompany this with breath and body work, such as tilting or jerking the head in different ways so that the remembrance is embodied. Such a practice can also bring to mind the story of how, in the beginning, God breathed divine breath into humans – indeed, into all of creation – giving them life. The sounds also serve as a kind of sonic meditation, recalling the scriptural accounts (both in the Qur'an and in Genesis) of how God created the elements of the world by speaking them into existence.

Asceticism and a name

Islam has always understood God's creation to be a good thing, and has not demanded asceticism of its followers. At the same time, it discourages a preoccupation with the pursuit of material goods and a life of luxury. "Everything that is on earth will perish," declares the Qur'an in words that echo similar verses in the Bible, "and the face of your Lord of majesty and honour will endure forever" (55:26–27). As the Prophet Muhammad exemplified in his own life, Islam can be seen as a middle way between the extremes of luxury and denial. Although he was the leader of the Muslim community, he lived in a simple home and refused to wear garments of majesty. Some traditions say that his wives complained to him that they did not have the fancy clothes of other women. Clearly, Muhammad sought no personal financial gains from his preaching.

However, in the second century of Islam (the eighth century CE), a rigorous asceticism rose up as a response to the worldliness that came with the political and economic power of the Umayyad Dynasty. As Islam spread into Persian and Byzantine territories, it came into contact with the wealth of both of those empires. As with the ascetic movement that accompanied the establishment of imperial Christendom in the fourth century, Muslim mystics rose up to keep Muslims faithful to the original vision of Islam in a context where wealth and power threatened to derail it.

A famous early Muslim ascetic was Hasan al-Basri, who died in 728. Traditions about him claim that he used to warn his hearers to live a life such that they would have no fear at the Hour of Judgment: "O son of Adam, you will die alone and enter the tomb alone and be resurrected alone, and it is with you alone that the reckoning will be made!" This quote reflects the idea that while people are responsible for their lives on earth, the things that they own and acquire in this life would not help them in the world to come. In another famous saying Hasan al-Basri compared the treasures of this world to a snake, whose scales were smooth to the touch but whose venom was deadly. He reminded his hearers that all of the treasures of the world were once offered to the Prophet Muhammad, who refused them. Muslims, therefore, should be content with "hunger for food, wool for a cloak, and their own feet for transportation."

Another early ascetic was Ibrahim ibn Adham, who died in 777. Ibn Adham is credited with classifying the three stages of asceticism: (1) renunciation of the world; (2) renunciation of the joy of having achieved that first renunciation; and (3) experience of the world as so unimportant as to be ignored. For Ibn Adham, asceticism extended to abstinence from sexual relations. In this respect, he was clearly outside of Islam's mainstream celebration of the heterosexual relationship of a married couple. Indeed, there is no official tradition of celibacy in Islam.

There were other ascetics in the time of the Umayyads. In 750, however, the Umayyad Dynasty was replaced by the Abbasids, who moved their headquarters to the city of Baghdad. There, courtly life emphasized public projects such as hospitals, schools, and the translation of Greek and Persian philosophical traditions into Arabic. This shift from a focus on wealth for the sake of empire to a focus on the empire's wealth existing for the sake of its inhabitants may have tempered the asceticism of the early Sufis. Another possible reason for the shift from asceticism was the life of the famous woman mystic, Rabi'a, who is described below. She is usually credited with introducing the metaphor of love into Sufism, thinking of God as the divine beloved.

Unitive mysticism

Although the term Sufism is etymologically connected with asceticism, the movement soon included a trajectory in the opposite direction. The early literature of Sufism stressed the development of moral qualities, particularly the humility that accompanied asceticism. The later tradition glorified the almost intoxicating pleasure of union with the divine. The metaphor was no longer that of being empty to reach God, but of being filled once you had the union with God. The language of sensuality overtook the language of asceticism.

Sometimes Sufis would express this yearning in such lofty terms that they were tragically misunderstood. Perhaps the most famous of these was Husayn ibn Mansur al-Hallaj (858–922), who expressed his union with God in the phrase "I am the Truth." To the pious and the conservatives around him, this statement smacked of blasphemy, suggesting that Al-Hallaj was claiming to be an equal with God. In the Islamic tradition, "the Truth" is one of the most beautiful names of God. Scholars since that time have concluded that Al-Hallaj was simply expressing a devout monotheism, claiming that God existed over all and in all, including himself. For his assertion, however, Al-Hallaj was put to death by the ruler of his time.

Many medieval Sufis would use the analogy of romantic love to describe their relationship with the Divine. Certainly the most famous of these was Jalal al-Din Rumi (1207–73), who was given the title of Maulana (our master). Rumi was born in the province of Balkh in what is now Afghanistan, and died in Konya, Turkey, but he is counted among the Persian poets, since he wrote in the Persian language. These days, when people in the West fear the Muslim conservatism in Afghanistan and Iran (ancient Persia) and worry about Turkey's bid to join the European Union, it is more important than ever to remember the legacy of Rumi.

At an early age, Rumi studied jurisprudence as well as the sciences of the Qur'an and the hadith. But a meeting with a mysterious stranger, Shams al-Din of Tabriz, ignited the creative spark within Rumi, allowing him to turn his attentions towards poetry. Rumi wrote two major books of poetry, the

Diwan (collected works) and the *Mathnawi* (couplets), as well as a number of other works. Through a number of English translations – most notably those of Coleman Barks – Rumi became the best-selling poet in the United States at the end of the twentieth century.

The *Mathnawi* begins with one of Rumi's most famous analogies, that of the reed. A flute maker plucks a reed from the reed bed and bores nine holes in it. This flute then plays a song of lament for having been separated from the reed bed. The analogy is clear: We are the reed whom God has plucked from the Garden of Eden. (Joni Mitchell's song "Woodstock" echoes a similar longing in its line "we've got to get ourselves back to the garden.") Rumi suggests that God has put holes in our bodies – eyes, ears, mouth, etc. – so that we can become instruments for divine music. It is not coincidental that the best pens for Islamic calligraphy are fashioned from the same cane reeds that are used for flutes. The flute playing a song of lament and the pen writing the divine words of the Qur'an thus embody the human longing for a return to the Garden of Eden and union with God.

Rumi composed many of his poems while circling a pillar in his home – one of his forms of *dhikr*. His disciples, therefore, came to be known as the Whirling Dervishes (*dervish* is related to the Persian word for "poor person" – another connection to the earlier asceticism). They were also known as the Mevlevi order, which has survived to this day. For a time in the twentieth century, when Turkey became aggressively secular, the order was forced underground, but now the Turkish government recognizes it as an important part of its national heritage. The order has made numerous tours of North America in recent years.

Philosophical Sufism

It would be wrong to assume that Sufism's emphasis on direct experience of the Divine meant that the movement was somehow anti-intellectual. The title *Shaykh al-Akbar* (the greatest master) was given to one of the most creative philosophical thinkers of any era, Muhyi al-Din ibn al-'Arabi (1165–1240). Ibn al-'Arabi was born in Islamic Spain, and died in Damascus. William Chittick, the greatest North American interpreter of Ibn al-'Arabi's thought, says that Ibn al-'Arabi: "wrote voluminously in Arabic prose and addressed every theoretical issue that arises in the context of Islamic thought and practice. His works are enormously erudite and exceedingly difficult, and only the most learned of Muslims, those already trained in jurisprudence, [theology], and other Islamic sciences, could have hoped to read and understand them."

I can relate to that assessment. When, as a graduate student at the University of Toronto, I read one of Ibn al-'Arabi's most famous books, the *Bezels of Wisdom*, I could read the Arabic words but often I could not understand the sentences that Ibn al-'Arabi had constructed. His ideas were too complex to be expressed by the existing language, and so he had to create his own forms of expression. One line, for example, translates as: "The names of God are infinite, for they are known by all of that which derives from them which is infinite, even though they derive from a fixed number of sources which are the enclosures or houses of the names." I still have no idea what that sentence means. The work speaks of the wisdoms (the word in the title is in plural form in the Arabic) of 27 different prophets, each of whose wisdom is likened to a different stone in the setting of a signet ring. Ibn al-'Arabi writes that the book was revealed to him in a vision of the Prophet Muhammad; it is understandable, then, that it might not be intelligible to someone who didn't share his vision. Even so, Ibn al-'Arabi's writing made me appreciate both the precision and the ambiguity of some mystical writing.

French scholar Henry Corbin also writes of the "imaginal" world that was central to Ibn al-'Arabi's thought. This was not some imaginary world of make-believe as some might understand the imagination. It is not the same as doing free associations of images in trying to understand, say, the birth of Jesus. Rather, it is a world available to religious visionaries, where spiritual truths are made real. Ibn al-'Arabi's vision of Muhammad, much like the Apostle Paul's vision of the risen Jesus, is on a higher plane. Dreams or visions are very important to all mystics, but for Sufis, meeting the Prophet in a vision is equal to meeting him in person. I believe that the English artist and poet, William Blake, resided in the imaginal world, occasionally coming out of it to the London where he lived and worked.

Another idea that is associated with Ibn al-'Arabi (although he himself never used the term) is sometimes translated as oneness, or unity of being — that all things borrow their existence from God. Seemingly disparate things can all, in their essence, be traced back to God. "My heart has become capable of all forms," he wrote in his cycle of poems entitled *The Interpreter of Desires*. "It is a pasture for gazelles, a cloister for monks, a temple for idols, the tablets of the Torah, the pilgrim's Ka'ba, and the manuscript of the Qur'an. It is the religion of love that I hold." This shows again how Sufism can be used to reconcile different traditions of animism, Christianity, polytheism, Judaism, and Islam. Within Islam, the idea that one could worship animals as gods, or worship other gods besides the one true God, is the most grievous sin, yet Ibn al-'Arabi seemingly presents these ideas without difficulty. While the heightened language of Ibn al-'Arabi's poetry might seem to extol animals and other created things as divine, beneath the surface it really celebrates the way the one true God fills and directs all of creation. Ibn al-'Arabi would still have considered it a sin to actually worship the creation rather than the Creator.

Sufism and orthodoxy

Muslim scholars have generally respected the writing and work of Sufism. One medieval Islamic theologian in particular, Abu Hamid al-Ghazali, did much to reconcile Sufism and orthodox Islam, showing that one could be a good Sufi and a good Muslim. Nevertheless, the relationship between Sufis and conservative or orthodox Muslims has always included some tension. It is true that Sufis sometimes appeared elite or gave the impression that they were not bound by the law incumbent on ordinary Muslims. However, many Sufis through history have understood their practices to be rooted in a deep understanding of the Qur'an and obedience to Islamic law. One cannot, for example, properly understand Rumi's poetry without a thorough understanding of the Qur'an and the hadith. Nonetheless, some orthodox Muslims have seen Sufism as being incompatible with "true" Islam.

For some of these conservatives, the issue is the veneration that Sufis pay to their teachers, particularly the founders of their orders. Often, Sufis would make their founders' tombs into shrines where they would pray for the founder's intervention in granting them well-being. Some orthodox Muslims see this as placing unnecessary intermediaries between the believer and God. At the beginning of the twentieth century, such criticism took an ugly turn when members of the conservative

Wahhabi movement in Saudi Arabia destroyed a number of important shrines.

Other critics are scandalized by the images used in certain Sufi writings, which can be quite erotic and sensual. Read literally, the writing is seen as pornographic rather than religious, in much the same way that the Song of Solomon can be experienced as erotic. Still other conservatives interpret some Sufi writings (like Ibn al-'Arabi's poem quoted above) as giving sanction to polytheism, the worst possible sin for Muslims.

One important fact that critics often ignore is that it was largely through the various Sufi orders that Islam spread. These orders were largely fixed after the death of al-Ghazali, so their theological orthodoxy was generally accepted. Some Sufis accompanied merchants in their travels, taking the message of Islam to far-flung areas of the world. Many would settle in particular areas, adapting to various cultural contexts and sharing their faith with those around them. Some served their communities as teachers, others as healers. They would not use coercion to convert people; instead, people were drawn to them.

Many Sufi orders continue to exist in the modern world, including several in North America. A number of major cities in North America are home to branches of the Shadhili order, as well as to Naqshbandi and Chishti orders. In a research project in 2004, I found Toronto to be home to seven different orders. There are also numerous Sufi retreat centres and communities across North America, offering spiritual seekers the option of attending regular meetings, going to retreats for a short period of time, or living in a Sufi community for an extended period. Interestingly, there are a few Sufi orders who see themselves as non-Muslim, meaning that they have separated themselves from the larger Islamic tradition. Indeed, I have met people who tell me that they are Sufi, but not Muslim.

Women and Sufism

Women have played an important role in the Sufi tradition, and have often served as positive role models for both men and women in Islam. This may also explain part of the historical tension between orthodox Islam and Sufism. One of the most famous of the early female Sufis, Rabi'a al-Adawiyya (713–801), is credited with introducing the metaphor of love into the Sufi tradition. Rabi'a believed that one should act only and always out of a love for God, not for fear of punishment or hope of a reward. One of the most beloved stories about her has her roaming the streets of her hometown, Basra, in Iraq. In her hands she carried a bucket of water and a flaming torch. When people asked her what she was doing, she said that with the bucket she would put out the fires of Hell, and with the torch she would set fire to the gardens of Paradise. That way, people would not worship God out of fear of being sent to Hell, or a desire to enter Paradise. They should worship God for the sake of worshipping God alone.

The Sufi tradition provided one of the few outlets for women to be recognized as leaders. Since the Sufis believed that one could achieve union with the Divine, who is without gender, one's own gender did not matter. After Rabi'a, women could be Sufi leaders even though they were prevented from being trained as imams. Also, the shrines of various Sufi saints, whether male or female, are often the preserve of women, a place where women have some measure of control. Women tend to be the caretakers of these shrines, and women often outnumber men at shrine gatherings, inverting the usual breakdown of attendance at mosques. Clearly, one can see how some men, used to public space being male space, might be threatened by a public space dominated by women.

Attitudes to peace and violence

Because of the nature of Sufism, it is not surprising that it includes a strong pacifist strain and a rejection of violence. Many of the early ascetics rejected the political, economic, and temporal power that was sought by many Islamic rulers. For other Sufis, particularly those who expressed their thought in the vocabulary of analogies, the union with the Divine left no room for war and hatred. Sufis were fond of quoting the sacred hadith where God says, "My mercy takes precedence over my wrath." Sufis understood God more in terms of love or beauty than in terms of power or majesty.

Unfortunately, this emphasis led many Islamic rulers to use Sufis as scapegoats. The execution of the mystic Al-Hallaj, who had declared his union with God, was a clear case. Was he really killed for being a "heretic?" Or was this another time in history when such persecution was a convenient means of deflecting public opinion and support away from the failures of the authorities? Was he really leading people away from God, or were the authorities simply looking to enhance their own power?

In the modern world, one sees Sufi influence in a number of peace groups. The largest Muslim pacifist group in North America is the Muslim Peace Fellowship, some of whose members are Sufis. Other Muslim pacifists join interfaith peace groups, such as the Fellowship of Reconciliation. In today's war-torn Iraq, Christian peacemaker teams from North America have partnered with, and helped to train, a similar network of

Muslim teams who try to build bridges between Sunnis and Shi'as and advocate for detainees.

A contemporary Sufi pacifist was M.R. Bawa Muhaiyaddeen, who was born in Sri Lanka but emigrated to the United States and lived in Philadelphia until his death in 1986. The mosque that he established is still active, as is a publishing program that spreads his teachings across North America. His book, *Islam and World Peace: Explanations of a Sufi*, situates issues of peace and justice within his own Sufi framework. He urged his followers to work for peace using non-violent means, saying that the only struggle (*jihad*) that should be waged is the internal one to make the person more submissive to God, thereby becoming a servant of fellow human beings.

Contemplative traditions as vehicles for dialogue

People of all religious traditions differ in their understandings of the Divine. Mystical traditions within the world's religions can be a vehicle for crossing over or transcending – not eliminating – these differences. Jews, Christians, and Muslims all believe that there is only one true God. Sufism has made a number of contributions to this search for common ground. For example, Sufi poetry is sometimes read on Christian spiritual retreats. Breathing exercises originating in the Naqshbandi Sufi order are sometimes used by Christian and Jewish contemplatives. Sufi music has made great inroads into world music. The work of Nusrat Fateh Ali Khan, for example, has achieved great crossover success. Khan collaborated with Eddie Vedder, the lead singer of the rock band Pearl Jam for two songs on the soundtrack to the motion picture *Dead Man Walking* about Sister Helen Prejean and the death penalty in America. Another example of interfaith appreciation of Sufism is the love that Jim

Strathdee, one of the most important musical leaders of the United Methodist Church, has for the works of Rumi.

Sufis are fond of quoting the saying, "Love the water more and the pitcher less." Too often, when people seek to quench their thirst, they focus on the outward form of the container that holds that water rather than on the water itself. Sufism and other mystical traditions challenge us to focus on the transcendent reality that the water represents, the ancient metaphor of the Water of Life, rather than remaining confined to our own separate understandings of God. In this way, the sum total of our collective worship is indeed greater than the individual traditions.

9

From tolerance to dialogue

Early in 2006, the global news media told of an Afghani man, Abdul Rahman, who was facing the death penalty for converting from Islam to Christianity. Some speculated that the charge of apostasy had been artificially raised to thwart his efforts to secure custody of his daughters. Many around the world sent messages of protest to the Afghanistan government, fearing that the case signalled new waves of human rights abuses in Afghanistan. He was released from prison in March of 2006 on the grounds that he was mentally unable to stand trial. Rahman – whose name ironically means "servant of the Merciful" – was soon given asylum in Italy. Even so, the legal issue of apostasy in Muslim society entered the consciousness of many people in the West.

Almost exactly five years earlier, Afghanistan had been in the news for another act of religious intolerance. In March 2001, the Taliban government blew up two giant statues of the Buddha carved into the cliffs of the Bamiyan region, claiming that the sculptures were an offence to Islam. A number of Muslim academics – myself included – signed a letter of protest when the decision to destroy the statues was announced. Egypt and

Iran, two countries with significant pre-Islamic monuments, sent delegations to plead with the Taliban not to destroy the statues. Representatives of The Organization of the Islamic Conference also travelled to Afghanistan to express their concern. Ironically, these delegations met in Kandahar, named after Alexander the Great, another pre-Islamic figure. Unfortunately, these calls were not heeded and the Buddhas of Bamiyan were destroyed. Today, the new the Afghani government has promised to rebuild the statues, with the help of UNESCO.

These two events raise issues around religious intolerance in a world where many, especially in the West, are opting for a culture of greater tolerance and religious pluralism. In this chapter we first examine Islamic attitudes towards apostasy, especially as related to the difficult verses in the Qur'an that might seem to support religious exclusivism. Then we will examine a number of aspects of Muslim and Christian faith that can help create bridges between them, including the figures of Mary and Jesus, and common commitments to peace and justice. Finally, in reviewing the many ways our civilizations have intersected historically, we will consider what religious pluralism might look like today.

Apostasy: turning away from Islam

Unfortunately, many Muslims and non-Muslims alike are unaware of the historical contexts that shaped the development of Islamic law. The harsh measures that some Muslims impose on those who leave the faith must be understood in light of Islam's beginnings as a persecuted tradition. As we saw in Chapters Three and Six, Muslims were threatened by the polytheists in Mecca, and a series of battles occurred between Muhammad's community in Medina and the polytheists of Mecca. In that context the death penalty as a punishment for apostasy was not so much a matter of religious affiliation as a matter of political identity. By reverting back to polytheism after having converted to Islam, one would actively be siding with the polytheists of Mecca and would therefore undermine the Muslim community. In effect, apostasy was comparable to treason, an offence which still carries the death penalty in several jurisdictions in the United States, though no longer in Canada.

In the modern period, extremist Muslims seem almost to take delight in applying those early precedents to apostates today. The classical jurists of Islamic law, however, were hesitant to rule on cases of apostasy, however, precisely because of the capital nature of the offence. They preferred to let God decide the matter on the day of judgment. Indeed, the Qur'an is clear that ultimate judgment belongs to God alone: "Whatever is in the heavens and whatever is in the earth belongs to God; God forgives whom God pleases and chastises whom God pleases; and God is Forgiving, Merciful" (3:129). This recourse to God's judgment is applied differently throughout the Muslim world; today some pacifist Muslims (discussed later in the chapter) take it so far as to renounce not only the death penalty but all violence in the defense of the faith. When Muslims take upon themselves God's role as judge of a person's faith, they flout the Qur'anic injunction given to the Prophet Muhammad himself, that he was to warn people but not force them to obey: "So therefore remind, for you [Muhammad] are one to remind, but you are not a warden over them. But whoever turns back and disbelieves, God will punish him with a mighty punishment. For to Us [God] is their return, and it will be for Us to call them to account" (88:21 – 26). It is therefore God who will inflict punishment when human beings return to God at the end of this life. Of course, Muslims believe that human beings still need law, or else there would be chaos. Even those of us who value human freedom agree that certain conventions such as traffic signals should be obeyed. The difficult issue is the intersection of human justice in this world with God's justice in the world to come.

Alliance and non-alliance: problematic verses

While Muhammad and his first followers were concerned mainly with polytheism, tensions with Jews and Christians were also present. Not surprisingly, while the Qur'an says many positive things about these traditions, it also includes critiques. For example, the following verse speaks against taking non-Muslims as friends: "Oh you who believe! Do not take the Jews and the Christians for friends; they are friends of each other; and whoever among you takes them for a friend, then surely he is one of them; surely God does not guide the unjust people" (5:51). Some Muslims have read this verse literally, and have chosen not to form friendships with Jews and Christians. However, this is clearly not the only way the verse can be interpreted, since many Muslims delight in their friendship with these people whom the Qur'an itself calls, respectfully, "People of the Book." The key phrase in the verse is a warning against "unjust people," suggesting that one should not befriend those who are unjust, whether they be Jews, Christians or Muslims.

A longer section from the Qur'an makes it clear that Muslims are to avoid those who are actively trying to cause them to compromise their faith in God or to distance themselves from their faith community. In the following quote are allusions to the polytheists who drove Muhammad and his community out of Mecca and to Abraham, who was called to leave his polytheistic family for the land of Canaan.

Oh you who believe! Do not take My [God's] enemy and
your enemy for friends: would you offer them love while
they deny what has come to you of the truth, driving
out the Messenger and yourselves because you believe
in God, your Lord? If you go forth struggling hard in
My path and seeking My pleasure, would you manifest
love to them? And I know what you conceal and what
you manifest; and whoever of you does this, he indeed
has gone astray from the straight path. If they find you,
they will be your enemies, and will stretch forth towards
you their hands and their tongues with evil, and they
ardently desire that you may disbelieve. Your relationship
would not profit you, nor your children on the day of
resurrection; God will decide between you; and God sees
what you do. Indeed, there is for you a good example in
Abraham and those with him when they said to their
people: 'Surely we are clear of you and of what you serve
besides God; we declare ourselves to be clear of you, and
enmity and hatred have appeared between us and you
forever until you believe in God alone' (60:1–4).

While the Qur'an upholds Abraham's example, it also contains
calls to Jews and Christians to uphold their own ideals. Again,
it is important to understand the context in which the Qur'an
was written. According to Islamic tradition, the Jews of Medina
sought to work with the pagan Meccans to overthrow the
Muslims. Thus, as the following quote shows, the people to be
avoided are "those among" the Children of Israel who rejected
their own faith:

Oh People of the Book! exceed not in your religion the
bounds, trespassing beyond the truth, nor follow the

vain desires of people who went wrong in times gone by – who misled many, and strayed from the right way. Curses were pronounced by the tongues of David and of Jesus the son of Mary on those among the Children of Israel who rejected faith, because they disobeyed and persisted in excesses… You see many of them turning in friendship to the unbelievers. Evil indeed is that which their souls have sent forward before them, so that God's wrath is on them, and in torment will they abide. If only they had believed in God, in the Prophet, and in what had been revealed to him, never would they have taken them for friends and protectors, but most of them are rebellious wrong-doers (5:77–81).

This was not a blanket condemnation on all Jews, but simply a reminder that they had been warned in the past against disobeying God and following their own selfish desires: Again, people are judged by the things that they do.

By contrast, the same passage goes on to praise Christians who – again in the context of the Arabian experience of the first Muslim community – seemed to share an affinity with the teachings of Muhammad:

Strongest among people in enmity to the believers will you find the Jews and Polytheists; and nearest among them in love to the believers will you find those who say, 'We are Christians': because among these are men devoted to learning and men who have renounced the world, and they are not arrogant. And when they listen to the revelation received by the Messenger, you shall see their eyes overflowing with tears, for they recognise the truth. They pray: 'Our Lord! we believe; write us down among the witnesses. What cause can we have not to believe in God and the truth which has come to us, seeing that we long for our Lord to admit us to the company of the righteous?' And for this their prayer God has rewarded them with gardens, with rivers flowing underneath, their eternal home. Such is the reward of those who do good (5:82 – 85).

Again, it is people who do evil works and who oppose the worship of the one God that are to be avoided, whether they be Jewish, Christian or Muslim.

There are also passages that are critical of Muslims who show disregard for others. Chapter 107, "The Small Kindness," expresses this admonishment in a nutshell:

In the Name of God the Compassionate the Merciful
Have you seen the one who calls the day of judgment a lie?
That is the one who treats the orphan harshly,
Who does not encourage the feeding of the needy.
Woe to those who pray,
Who are unmindful of their prayers.
Those who would be seen,
But refuse the small kindness.

It should be clear from these verses that everyone will be judged by God; no one group of people has a guaranteed ticket to heaven. Muslims must behave appropriately, and those who do not will be punished by God. Conversely, non-Muslims who do the right things, worship God, and observe their duties to the people around them will be rewarded by God.

Verses of alliance and dialogue

In a remarkable passage, the Qur'an speaks about the creation of humanity, and about which people are better than others: "O humanity! Truly We [God] created you from a male and a female, and made you into nations and tribes that you might know each other. Truly the most honoured of you in the sight of God is the most God-conscious of you. Truly God is Knowing, Aware" (49:13). There are four key points in this verse. First, the passage is addressed to all of humanity, not only to Muslims. Second, the passage mentions that the creation of humanity into distinct groupings comes from God and is a positive value. Third, it encourages people to transcend their differences and learn from each other. Finally, the passage does not say that Muslims are by definition better than other people, but that the best people are those who are aware of God.

The Qur'an affirms that interfaith relationships are possible, and offers some principles of interfaith behaviour. In 5:48, for example, God says: "For every one of you did we appoint a law and a way, and if God had pleased, God would have made you a single people, but that God might try you in what God gave you, therefore strive with one another to hasten to virtuous deeds; to God you will all return, so God will let you know that in which you differed." Again, in 2:147–148, "The Truth is from your Lord; so be not at all in doubt. To each is a goal to which God turns them; then strive together towards all that is good. Wherever you are, God will bring you together. For God has power over all things." Finally, 2:256 states that "there is no compulsion in religion, truth stands clear from error," clearly opposing forced or coerced conversion and in favour of interfaith dialogue among people who also worship one God.

People of the Book. In the Qur'an, Muslims are continually reminded of their relationship with the "People of the Book" *(ahl al-kitab)* – those who have received an earlier revelation from God. Most Muslims understand these people to include Christians, Jews, and Zoroastrians. The Qur'an allows that Muslims and the People of the Book may eat together, and that Muslim men may marry Jewish, Christian, or Zoroastrian women: "This day the good things are allowed to you; the food of those who have been given the Book is lawful for you and your food is lawful for them; and also the chaste from among the believing women and the chaste from among those who have been given the Book before you; when you have given them their dowries and married them, not fornicating with them or taking them for secret concubines" (5:5). This verse speaks to our earlier discussion about friendship. How can one think that Muslims cannot befriend Jews and Christians if they are encouraged to eat together and intermarry?

Another Qur'anic verse is even more explicit about the righteousness of faithful Jews and Christians and the reward of such righteousness: "Some of the People of the Book are a wholesome nation. They recite God's signs in the watches of the night, prostrating themselves, having faith in God and the last day, bidding to honour and forbidding dishonour, and vying with one another in good deeds. They are among the wholesome. Whatever good they do, they will not be denied its reward" (3:113–115). The Qur'an, therefore, envisions a peaceful coexistence that comes from a common revelation and a common God. If they do come into conflict, then they should remember the common God that they worship. "Argue not with the People of the Book" we are told, "unless it be in a better way, except with such of them as do wrong; and say: 'We believe in that which has been revealed to us and revealed to you; our God and your God is One, and to God do we surrender'" (29:46).

Polytheists. The Qur'an is not nearly as conciliatory toward people other than the People of the Book. Since Islam is a strictly monotheistic religion, Muslims believe that the most grievous sin is polytheism, or the worship of gods other than the one true God. Muslims have often had strained or hostile relationships with polytheists and atheists, just as Christians have in their history (for example, in their early relationship with "pagan" indigenous peoples of North America). It was in the context of the warfare between the polytheists of Mecca and Muhammad's community in Medina that the following verses were revealed: "But when the forbidden months are past then fight and slay the polytheists wherever you find them" (9:5). However, since those early years of establishing the Muslim community, Muslims and polytheists have managed to co-exist in many settings. The country with the largest number of Muslims is Indonesia, where the dominant religious traditions before Islam were Hinduism and Buddhism, indigenous traditions, and Dutch Christianity. The Muslims who spread Islam in Indonesia did not conduct a wholesale slaughter of "pagans" in the country.

The country with the third-largest Muslim population is India. Both within India and between India and Pakistan, sectarian hatred and violence is a sad reality. However, much of the violence between Hindus, Muslims, Sikhs, and Christians in India shows religion being used as a powerful political symbol and force. As in other areas of sectarian violence, such as Northern Ireland, demagogues and other power-hungry political figures use religion to incite people against each other for what may be economic or political grievances.

In India, where Hindus are the majority, it is often Hindus who have done the persecuting. One might recall the 2002 news story of a fire on a train in the state of Gujarat, where 59 Hindus were killed. Muslims were initially blamed for setting the fire, but this was disputed. In retaliation, Hindu mobs killed hundreds of Muslims and displaced thousands of others. The Muslim minority provided a convenient scapegoat for the majority, and with their displacement, their land and property could be confiscated and turned over to the supporters of the government. In other parts of India, however, one finds more peaceful coexistence. In the north, there are great similarities between Hindus and Muslims in terms of dance, music, food, movies, ritual, attachment to family, worship, and notions of a just civil life. Many Muslims and Hindus have good interfaith relationships, and the polytheism of many Hindus does not keep Indian Muslims from relating to them. In my own life, I have been privileged to have good relationships with my Hindu friends.

The Qur'an is clear in commanding Muslims to always act out of justice, and not out of hate: "Oh you who believe! Be upright for God as witnesses to justice, and let not hatred of a people incite you to not act equitably; act equitably, that is nearer to piety, and observe your duty to God. Surely God is aware of what you do" (5:8). Muslims are therefore called to treat people on the basis of how they behave, not because they identify themselves as Muslims, monotheists, or polytheists. While some Muslims have been extremely intolerant and violent towards other people – including other Muslims – it is important to remember that Muslims as a rule try to take seriously the call to coexist peacefully with their non-Muslim neighbours.

Exclusive and inclusive views

In both the Christian and Muslim communities there are large groups who believe that it is only in their particular faith that salvation is found. Some conservative Christians and Muslims have no interest in dialogue – only in debate and in conversion to their particular tradition. But one must be careful not to assume that all Christians and Muslims are of that mind. For example, since the Second Vatican Council, the Roman Catholic Church – while officially holding that there is not salvation outside the church – has taught that the Church rejects nothing that is true and holy in the great world religions. Indeed, it recognizes that their rules and teachings "often reflect a ray of that Truth which enlightens all men." One of the documents that came out of that council, *Lumen Gentium* (Light of Nations), specifically mentions Islam: "But the plan of salvation also includes those who acknowledge the Creator, in the first place among whom are the Muslims: these profess to hold the faith of Abraham, and together with us they adore the one, merciful God, mankind's judge on the last day."

An even more inclusive vision is shared by the United Church of Canada, the largest Protestant Church in Canada. In 2004, the United Church published a study document entitled *That We May Know Each Other: United Church—Muslim Relations Today*. The subtitle of the document was indicative of its goal: "Toward a United Church of Canada understanding of the relationship between Christianity and Islam in the Canadian context."[1] In 2005, I led a weekend workshop on this document at Trinity–St. Paul's United Church in Toronto, where I am a non-Christian adherent. Raheel Raza, a Muslim woman author and interfaith activist gave the sermon at the Sunday worship service.

The study document was designed to pave the way for acceptance of a denominational statement on the relationship of the United Church to Muslims in Canada. The proposed statement began with an acknowledgement of the history of Christian hostility and misunderstanding toward Muslims, and ended with invitations for faithful dialogue and a way for both groups to "seek justice and resist evil." Trinity – St. Paul's United Church endorsed the proposed statement. (At the time of writing, the General Council had not yet met to give a denominational response to the statement, but it was anticipated that it would have broad support.)

North American Muslims have also pursued interfaith relationships. African American

God reaches out to everyone

At the University of Toronto, I completed my PhD dissertation on Muslim communities in Toronto under the supervision of the late Professor Willard Oxtoby. In addition to being an academic, he was an ordained Presbyterian minister who also represented an inclusive view of Christianity. He ended one of his books, *The Meaning of Other Faiths* with the following words: "At no time have I ever thought of myself as anything other than a Christian. At no time have I ever supposed that God could not adequately reach out to me, to challenge and to comfort, in my own Christian faith and community. Yet at no time have I ever supposed that God could not also reach out to other persons in their traditions and communities as fully and as satisfyingly as he has to me in mine. At no time have I ever felt I would be justified in seeking to uproot an adherent of another tradition from his faithful following of that tradition. My Christianity – including my sense of Christian ministry – has commanded that I be open to learn from the faith of others." I would hope that we can all have something of Oxtoby's openness, and that those of us who are religious can believe that God works not just in our own communities of faith, but in all others as well.

Muslims, who make up at least 25 percent of American Muslims, have been especially active. I cannot think of a single African American mosque that has not had substantial outreach to Christians. After the devastation of Hurricane Katrina in 2005, the mosque led by Imam Mahmoud Abdul Rauf in Gulfport, Mississippi, did substantial work with other communities of faith to help the victims.

In the area of dialogue, I think of many examples. The American Islamic Congress, under the leadership of Harvard University Professor Ali Asani, publishes a "Guide to Muslim Interfaith Dialogue" which is distributed to Muslims through mosques. In Los Angeles, the Islamic Center of Southern California has also done a tremendous amount of interfaith work with Jewish and Christian communities. Finally, early in 2006 when the Ismaili community in Los Angeles marked the birthday of the Prophet Muhammad, one of the event's keynote speakers was Karen Torjesen, a Christian who is the Dean of the School of Religion at Claremont Graduate University. In her remarks, she wondered if a Muslim had similarly been invited to talk about Jesus at a Christian service on Christmas.

Besides denominational statements and conversations over recent years, Christians and Muslims committed to social justice have often found common ground with each other. One thinks, for example, of the excellent work that Mennonite Central Committee (MCC) has done with Palestinians, both in North America and in Israel/Palestine. MCC has sponsored interfaith delegations among North Americans, Palestinians, and Israelis so that people can learn more about the conflict. They have helped to teach Palestinians (85 percent of whom are Muslim) about conflict resolution, and have helped to teach Israelis about the injustices that Palestinians have experienced. MCC has also helped with several relief projects in Palestine.

On this continent, Muslims can be found serving Christians and serving alongside Christians in their works of social service and charity. In Toronto, they work in interfaith efforts to shelter the homeless during winter. In Los Angeles, the Islamic Center of Southern California has started a food bank to feed the homeless in the area, almost all of whom are non-Muslims. For many of the homeless who are served, it is their first time inside a mosque. It is these people, who do not simply engage in interfaith dialogue as an intellectual exercise, but also find themselves called to make a difference in the lives of others, who represent the inclusive spirit at work. Exclusive views can help some in our own community, while inclusive views can make for a more just world for all.

Jesus as a focal point

Another bridge toward inclusivity is the regard that both Christians and Muslims have for Jesus, Mary, John the Baptist, and Zechariah (the father of John), all of whom are mentioned in the Qur'an. Jesus, in particular, is an important prophet for Muslims, and is mentioned in 15 chapters and 93 verses of the Qur'an. It may surprise Christians that Muslims have collected more than 300 sayings of Jesus over the centuries. Tarif Khalidi's *The Muslim Jesus: Sayings and Stories in Islamic Literature* (see "Suggestions for Further Reading" on page 218) brings these together from "scattered works of ethics and popular devotion, belles-lettres, works of Sufism, anthologies of wisdom, and histories of prophets and saints." Many Muslims are familiar with several of these sayings. My own favourite is this one: "Jesus was asked, 'Spirit and Word of God, who is the most seditious of men?' He replied, 'The scholar who is in error. If a scholar errs, a host of people will fall into error because of him.'"

Jesus therefore serves as a focal point for Christian-Muslim dialogue in a way that he does not in Christian-Jewish dialogue. Even though Jesus was Jewish, he is not recognized in any significant way by the Jewish tradition. Muslims, however, agree with Christians about the importance of Jesus, even though they differ greatly on what they believe about Jesus. These differences are nevertheless points of discussion that can bring Christians and Muslims together in meaningful dialogue that, if done right, can be respectful and fruitful.

There are some key points of convergence and divergence around their views of Jesus. Although Muslims believe that Jesus was born of Mary, a virgin, they do not believe this made him divine. The Qur'an is explicit on this point: "They disbelieve who say 'God is Christ, the son of Mary.' Christ said: 'Oh Children of Israel, serve God, my Lord and your Lord. Whoever joins other gods with God, God has forbidden them the garden, their dwelling shall be the fire. There will be no helpers for those who do wrong'" (5:72). While Muslims accept Christ as Messiah, they do not believe that he is divine. In this way, Muslims are like Jews, thinking that the Christian doctrine of the Trinity detracts from a pure monotheism. Some Muslims have misunderstood Christian doctrine to think that Christians worship three gods, but this is an incorrect interpretation of the Trinity.

In the Qur'an, Jesus is described by many names. Most often, he is referred to by his proper name, Jesus. The title "Son of Mary" occurs 23 times in the Qur'an, but only once in the New Testament (Mark 6:3). Other designations are: servant of God; prophet; messenger; word; spirit; sign; example; witness; a mercy; eminent; brought near to God; upright; and blessed. A number of miracles are also associated with Jesus. In addition to speaking from the cradle as an infant, he creates birds from clay and they come to life and fly away (reminiscent of a story from the apocryphal *Infancy Gospel of Thomas*). Jesus heals the blind and the lepers; raises the dead; and feeds his followers from a heavenly table.

Eleven times, the Qur'an also refers to Jesus as "messiah." or "anointed one" – a direct parallel with the same term in Hebrew. The word *messiah* is translated into Greek as Christ, and thus assumes divine significance. But the differences between Christian and Muslim usages of term are significant. Unlike Christians, when Muslims think of Jesus as "messiah" or "Christ," they do not think of Jesus as God, or God incarnate. "The messiah, Jesus son of Mary, was only the messenger of God, and God's word that God committed to Mary, and a spirit from God" (4:169). Naturally, then, Muslims do not believe that Jesus is our Saviour. Like Jews, Muslims do not believe in the notion of original sin, and so do not think that we need to be saved by Jesus' death. Like Jews, Muslims also do not believe that someone else can atone for our sins, and so do not believe that Jesus was sacrificed for our sins. The Qur'an even denies that Jesus was crucified on the cross.

But like the New Testament, the Qur'an does portray Jesus as a prophet of social justice. This comes through in a charming story of how Mary was once criticized by some in her community who could not accept the virgin birth of Jesus. In the story, Mary points to the child, indicating that he should speak for himself. "But they said, 'How shall we speak to one who is still in the cradle, a little child?' Jesus said, 'Behold, I am God's servant; God has given me the book and made me a prophet. God has made me blessed, wherever I may be; and God has enjoined me to pray and to give alms so long as I live, and likewise to cherish my mother; God has not made me arrogant or unblessed. Peace be upon me the day I was born, and the day I die, and the day I am raised up alive'" (Qur'an 19:30-35). Jesus thus reflects a call to action and social justice; one must pray and take care of the poor.

Clearly, there are both points of agreement as well as substantial differences between Muslim and Christian understandings of Jesus, as well as the relationship between Jesus and God. But the esteem in which both faith communities hold Jesus should keep them in dialogue. Another document from the Second Vatican Council expresses well the search for common understanding. *Nostra Aetate* (In Our Time), proclaimed by His Holiness Pope Paul VI on October 28, 1965, declared:

> The Church has also a high regard for the Muslims. They worship God, who is one, living and subsistent, merciful and almighty, the Creator of heaven and earth, who has spoken to men. They strive to submit themselves without reserve to the hidden decrees of God, just as Abraham submitted himself to God's plan, to whose faith Muslims eagerly link their own. Although not acknowledging him as God, they venerate Jesus as a prophet, his Virgin Mother they also honor, and even at times devoutly invoke. Further, they await the day of judgment and the reward of God following the resurrection of the dead. For this reason they highly esteem an upright life and worship God, especially by way of prayer, alms-deeds and fasting.

In turn, Muslims have issued similar statements regarding their common ground with Christians. In 2005, a number of Muslim and Christian scholars and clerics from Egypt, Lebanon, Iraq, Palestine, and Jordan met in Cairo for a three-day forum on interfaith dialogue. At that forum, Shaykh Muhammad al-

Tantawi, the leader of Al-Azhar University, said. "The origin of all celestial religions is one, and their message is one, and that is to propagate virtue, good behaviour, and obedience to God." The same year, North America's largest Sunni organization, the Islamic Society of North America (ISNA), sent condolences to the Vatican on the death of His Holiness Pope John Paul II. In its statement of welcome to the new Pope , the ISNA promised:

> We will continue to cooperate, build alliances, promote dialogue and strengthen conversations with the Roman Catholic Church in accordance with Qur'anic injunctions to seek common grounds with the 'People of the Book.' We hope and pray that the Roman Catholic Church will continue to advance the cause of peace and justice for people of all faiths under the leadership of Pope Benedict XVI, building upon John Paul II's legacy of interfaith outreach and reconciliation based on mutual respect and religious tolerance.

Pluralism

The challenge of dialogue is closely related to what has become a key characteristic of Western society: pluralism. But let me be clear about what I mean by the word. First, pluralism is not the same thing as diversity. People from different religions and ethnic backgrounds may be present in one place, but unless they are involved in a constructive engagement with one another, there is no pluralism. In other words, pluralism is the positive value we place on diversity. Second, the goal of pluralism is not simply tolerance of the other, but rather an active attempt to arrive at an understanding. One can, for example, tolerate a neighbour about whom one remains thoroughly ignorant. Third, pluralism is not the same thing as relativism. Far from simply ignoring the profound differences among and within religious traditions, pluralism is committed to engaging the very differences that we have, to gain a deeper sense of each other's commitments. This, for me, is the goal of interfaith dialogue – not that we seek to convert each other, but that we help each other to find what is meaningful in our own traditions.

North American Muslims are in a position to influence the rest of the Muslim world in a way that opens doors toward pluralism. In countries where Muslims are in the majority, people of other religious traditions often suffer restriction, and sometimes persecution. Baha'is in Iran and Christians in Pakistan, for example, have been harassed, had their property taken, and even imprisoned for their activities. It is easy to be taught to hate these groups when they are such small minorities. As a religious minority, we North American Muslims can show our co-religionists what pluralism is. Here, we can live safely and securely, practicing our faith without having to convert or torment our non-Muslim neighbours (or for that matter, Muslims who aren't "Muslim enough" for the self-righteous). The stereotypes that we may have learned (for example that Christians worship three gods and are therefore polytheistic) fall away when we are invited to a Christian worship service and realize that we are worshipping the same one God.

In order to do interfaith dialogue properly, one must have not only a deep understanding of one's own faith, but also an understanding and appreciation of the faith of the dialogue partner. This can only be done in a pluralistic context, where it is possible to have a deep knowledge of more than one faith. I believe that accepting pluralism is a sign of firm faith and confidence, not a sign of doubt. We as North American Muslims need to commit ourselves to pluralism, not because we have to but because we should. It is part of the vision imparted to us by the Qur'an and the example of the Prophet.

North American Muslims can also model dialogue within the Muslim community. All too often, this is a neglected aspect of religious dialogue. In Toronto, I as a Sunni had the profound privilege of sometimes saying the Friday afternoon prayer side-by-side with a Shi'a colleague in a mosque built by Albanians, led by a Bosnian imam. In other parts of the Muslim world, this would be almost unthinkable, especially where there is sectarian violence between Sunnis and Shi'as.

Particularly in this era of frequent religious conflict, Muslims have a great opportunity to return to the pluralistic vision of the Qur'an, and to establish co-operative relations with other religious communities. As we have seen, the Qur'an declares that God deliberately chose not to create a humanity with no differences. In fact, the Qur'an speaks about God willing our differences and our disputes: "We [God] have made some of these messengers to excel the others; among them are they to whom God spoke, and some of them God exalted by rank. And We gave clear miracles to Jesus the son of Mary, and strengthened him with the holy spirit. If God had pleased, those after them would not have fought one with another after clear arguments had come to them, but they disagreed; so there were some of them who believed and others who denied. And if God had pleased, they would not have fought one with another, but God brings about what God intends" (2:253). Our differences and ensuing disputes are not to be feared, denied or eradicated. God teaches us through our differences. It is through dialogue that we learn about ourselves, about others, and in so doing, perhaps also about God.

It is also through dialogue that North Americans will appreciate the important Islamic roots of Western civilization. Much of the Greek philosophical tradition was preserved by the Arab Muslim world. In the Middle Ages, Aristotle was known as the pre-eminent philosopher in Europe and the Muslim world, but an Arab Muslim named al-Farabi was the pre-eminent commentator on Aristotle. Muslim philosophers Ibn Rushd and Ibn Sina – Latinized as Averroes and Avicenna – are critical to understanding Western philosophy in the Middle Ages. Arabic translations of Greek texts were once more translated into Latin and read by the thinkers who would begin the Renaissance. One cannot understand the European tradition of lyric and epic poetry without examining the Muslim roots of that tradition.

Muslim contributions to science, medicine, and mathematics are better known in the West than the Muslim preservation and continuation of the Greek philosophical tradition. Early Arab Muslim rulers brought together Muslim and non-Muslim scientists and scholars from various parts of the Muslim world in a common pursuit of knowledge. We call our numbers Arabic numbers, and we use them in place of Roman numerals. Arab Muslim mathematicians brought the concept of zero from India, and transmitted it to the European world. European medical schools used Arabic anatomy texts until the late middle ages. Algebra and algorithm are but two of the many scientific words that have their roots in the names of Muslim scholars.

Muslims and Christians thus share a common civilization. Indeed, some Christians may have more in common theologically with some Muslims than with other Christians. The reverse is also true for Muslims who may find the behaviour of their Christian neighbours to be more "muslim" (in the literal sense of living a life of submission to God) than that of some of their fellow Muslims. Through dialogue, we can begin to understand our common heritage, which can lead us to work together on a common future.

10

Paths of coexistence in a shared future

As the first person in my family to go to university, I often felt lost in my first year at the University of Toronto. One of my classes was in a building called Northrop Frye Hall. There, I would see a bust of the man after whom the building was named. One day, coming out of another building, I saw a man who looked exactly like the bust. I knew that if a living member of this 150-year-old university community had a building named after him, he must be very important. I discreetly asked some of my academically-seasoned residence mates if they knew who this person was. They told me that he was one of the most brilliant English professors in North America, famous for his courses on Shakespeare and for his course, "The Mythological Framework of Western Culture."

Through his courses, conversation, and writing, the late Professor Frye turned out to be an important figure in my approach to interfaith issues. He taught me about the power of myths, the stories that give meaning to our lives. Most people think of a myth either as a story that is false, or as a way for "primitive" peoples to explain their understanding of the world.

Myth is somehow pitted against scientific knowledge. But this is not how Frye understood the term. To him, a myth was a story that is true because it helps to give meaning to our lives. Myths are told in the language of metaphor and symbol, which make sense at deep levels of our being. Frye's first book, *Fearful Symmetry*, illustrated the power of myth at work in the literature of English poet and artist, William Blake. To understand Blake, one has to understand the symbolic world that he had created which, in turn, was deeply rooted in the Bible.

Through my study of Blake in the courses taught by Frye as well as by Jerry and Beth Bentley, I came to understand and love the Bible. I went on to study other mythological literature (as defined by Frye) and grew to understand the importance of learning each other's stories in order to create new stories, or to imagine old stories anew. I found that this process, which I stumbled upon almost by accident, was something that one of Frye's successors, J. Edward Chamberlin, advocated in his book *If This is Your Land, Where are Your Stories?*

Theology involves the study of some of our most important stories: our stories about God. In his book *The Heart of Christianity*, Bible scholar and church historian Marcus Borg discusses the story of Christianity. He tells of two different versions of that story – the "earlier" paradigm and the "emerging" paradigm. The first paradigm involves a belief in the Bible as a unique book from God, intended to be read literally. It also makes the afterlife a central concern of faith. This paradigm still gives meaning to millions of North American Christians.

Millions of other Christians, however, are not satisfied with this traditional understanding. The emerging paradigm, says Borg, can be described by five adjectives: *historical, metaphorical,* and *sacramental* with regard to Christian tradition; and *relational* and *transformational* with respect to Christian life. This paradigm is meaningful to Christians who look to the Bible as a human product, shaped in particular historical contexts, using particular languages and metaphors to help us understand something of the sacred. In the emerging paradigm, the central focus is on our relationship with God and the transforming power of that relationship in our earthly lives. One does not have to believe in the literal truth of such tenets as the virgin birth of Jesus or the blood atonement of Jesus to live in a way that is consistent with the ethical teachings of Jesus.

I have written this book for Christians who follow either the earlier or the emerging paradigm. In this concluding chapter, I describe how Muslims are seeking to understand their religious tradition, and how they can coexist with Christians. Crucial in this exercise is an understanding of our own stories and an openness to learn from other stories. Before exploring how Borg's work could lead to changes in the way Muslims understand their tradition, and in how Muslims and Christians relate to each other, however, I begin with a story that helps illustrate the spirit of such interfaith learning.

The story of Wilfred Cantwell Smith

Wilfred Cantwell Smith was the greatest North American scholar of Islam, and the most important Canadian scholar of religion in the 20th century. Born in 1916, he earned an undergraduate degree in Oriental Studies at the University of Toronto, then did graduate work in Cambridge, England, before traveling to Lahore, India (today part of Pakistan). Here, he and his wife Muriel studied for six years before the end of British colonial rule and the partition of India into India and Pakistan.

Following World War II and doctoral studies at Princeton University, Smith came to McGill University in Montreal where, in 1951, he founded and directed the Institute for Islamic Studies. Here he brought Muslim and non-Muslim scholars together to study Islam. In 1964 he went to Harvard University to direct the Center for the Study of World Religions, a post he held for two decades. I was privileged to get to know him and Muriel when they retired to their native Toronto in 1985. He was a Fellow of the American Academy of Arts and Sciences, and a month before his death in February 2000, he was inducted into the Order of Canada.

At the beginning of Smith's career, the study of Islam consisted almost entirely of the study, by non-Muslim scholars, of texts written by Muslims. Raised in Canada when there were very few Muslims in his country, he felt compelled to spend time in India, which before its partition was the country with the largest number of Muslims. To live with Muslims, to actually get to know them and learn their stories, was a revolutionary idea at the time.

One of Smith's gifts was that he was able to learn the stories in their original languages. He came from a time and social class where he learned English, French, Greek, and Latin in high school. He learned Arabic, Hebrew, and Persian in university. In India, he studied Sanskrit and Pali. When I knew him, he could talk with me fluently in my own mother tongue, Urdu. It was from that deep knowledge of many languages and stories, gained through scholarship and personal experience, that he was able to write about the lives of people from other cultures.

Smith's thinking revolutionized the study of religion. "Religion," he wrote, "is best understood as the living, vital faith of individual persons rather than as an abstract set of ideas and doctrines." But this is only one of the reasons that his example is important for us. Smith also had a tremendous sense of social concern, rooted both in his scholarship and in his moral outlook, both of which were incredibly rigorous.

His study of Islam in India, for example, touched on the problems of the British colonization of that country. His first book, *Modern Islam in India*, published in 1946, argued that the British should leave India. He initially submitted the manuscript to Cambridge University as a dissertation. As he must have anticipated, however, the dissertation was rejected; Cambridge was, after all, the premier university for training the British elite, which had the most to gain from colonialism. In the end, he wrote a completely different dissertation on a different topic when he earned his PhD at Princeton University. From this early example, however, we see his unwavering commitment to justice. He was prepared to speak the truth to power, despite the negative consequence it might have on his own life.

Professor Smith was neither a Muslim nor an apologist for Islam. At the same time, he could respectfully criticize Muslims in a way that never did violence to what their religion meant to them. (This is crucial to the serious interfaith dialogue that is needed in our day; one must never misrepresent the views of one's dialogue partner.) In 1957, he wrote in *Islam in Modern History*: "A true Muslim... is not a man who believes in Islam – especially Islam in history; but one who believes in God and is committed to the revelation through His Prophet." Five years later, in *The Meaning and End of Religion*, he continued: "The essential tragedy of the modern Islamic world is the degree to which Muslims, instead of giving their allegiance to God, have been giving it to something called Islam." Those words could have been written yesterday with equal force and validity.

Professor Smith's life-long work was to show that the core of being religious is a matter of personal faith – not propositional belief or allegiance to institutions. His son, Brian Cantwell Smith, now Dean of the Faculty of Information Studies at the University of Toronto recounts this incident with his father: "'I'm not going to go to church anymore!' I announced, upon returning home for Christmas after my first year in college; 'I just don't believe all that stuff!' (I was 17). 'Well,' he said – with his trademark pause – 'that's probably right, if they are asking you for dogmatic assent. Focussing on agreement is a recent trend, only 150 years old or so; it is going to be the death of the church. The problem you will find, though, is that, by opting out of religious community, you will lose the vocabulary in terms of which to talk to your closest friends about the things that matter to you most.'"

Smith made explicit the distinction between "faith" and "cumulative tradition" – two realities that the believing person links together. For Smith, faith through much of history has been an individual's personal piety, or what Muslims understand as *iman* (faith) or *taqwa* (awareness of God). Until the seventeenth century, *religion* was the term that was given to this personal orientation to the divine. Since then, the term has come to mean a particular doctrine or set of doctrines. Personal piety is distinct from the accumulation of the religious materials of a tradition, such as texts, buildings, laws, rituals, and art – traditions that evolve and change over time and across cultures, even while God remains eternal. The distinction between tradition and personal faith, therefore, helps us to understand Islam as the particular faith of particular Muslims, not as an abstract concept.

How might Smith's analysis help the current search for greater understanding among faiths, particularly between

Muslims and Christians? For me, it is the plurality that comes as we talk about personal faith – our own and that of our dialogue partners. Sharing on this level will be much more fruitful than trying to treat faith – whether Muslim or Christian – as some kind of monolithic, impersonal theory.

What Muslims can learn from Christians

In the media these days many people seem to be calling for an Islamic reformation, led by an Islamic Martin Luther. I view such calls with deep suspicion – and not simply because I teach at a university run by Catholics, whose history includes the resistance toward the Protestant Reformers. Both as a scholar and as a religious person I am puzzled by the idea that one religious tradition should develop the same way as another.

As a scholar I am in many ways a traditionalist; I see myself as one who is steeped in the past, who always tries to respect and honour my elders. With roots in a working class family, I have had the privilege of learning from some of the finest scholars in the world. In no way could I even begin to match the work of my teachers, let alone surpass them. My personal academic motto is a saying of Confucius: "I am a transmitter, not an innovator, and a lover of the ancients."

As a Muslim, I am also wary of religious innovation. The Prophet said on a number of occasions that good innovations will be rewarded, but bad innovations that misguide people will be punished with hell. In these pages, I am not asking Muslims to do anything new. Rather, I am reminding them to understand the complexity of their cumulative tradition, and return to their faith. As Smith did, I am calling them to worship God instead of Islam.

Can Muslims learn from Borg's "earlier" and "emerging" paradigms of Christianity? Yes, but not in exactly the same pattern as in Christianity. The developments in Christianity do not have the same meaning in Islam. For example, the emerging paradigm looks at the Bible not as the words of God, but as a human response to God. The composition of the Bible involved multiple authors writing in different geographical locations over very long periods of time. In the complex process of establishing the choice of writings to be included, a number of apocryphal texts were excluded, although they were used by various Christian groups for centuries afterwards. The history of the Qur'an is very different. For Muslims, a fundamental assumption is that the Qur'an is the direct words of God through one person, Muhammad. The Qur'an was revealed in a much smaller geographical space over the course of a little more than two decades.

The authority of scripture is therefore seen differently in the two traditions. However, Muslims can benefit from the emerging paradigm by understanding the Qur'an in its historical and cultural contexts – asking when and why and how the verses were revealed to Muhammad. They can also learn about the truth of metaphor. Just as more and more Christians see the truth of the Bible to be in the way it provides meaning for their lives and puts them in touch with the Divine, so Muslims can experience "truth" in new ways. What once might have been understood as literally true is now seen as metaphorically true. The Qur'an seems to give some allowance for such understandings. "It is God who has revealed the Book to you," says 3:7, "In it are clear revelations which are the foundation of the Book, while others are metaphorical." The Qur'an then warns against people who lead others astray by reading the metaphorical verses literally.

Another point of convergence is in the area of lifestyle and ethics. "The emerging paradigm," Borg writes, "sees the Christian life as a life of relationship and transformation."

This works perfectly for Muslim life as well. For Muslims, a relationship with God should lead to a transformed life, lived in and for the service of God.

One of my favourite stories about Wilfred Cantwell Smith could apply equally as well to Muslims as to Christians. A student, not knowing that Professor Smith was an ordained Presbyterian minister, asked him: "Professor Smith, are you Christian?" If the question had been "Are you *a* Christian?" the answer would have been a simple yes. Instead, the question required a deeper answer. Professor Smith thought for a moment, and repeated the question, "Am I Christian? I don't know, maybe I was, last week, on a Tuesday, at lunch, for about an hour. But if you really want to know, ask my neighbour." To Professor Smith, it was clear that his Christian identity was best measured by how he treated the people around him, by living his life in an integrated whole.

Muslims can also learn a great deal from Christians about developing their religious communities in North America. Muslims have worked on the first phase, which is the establishment of places of worship. There are now a large number of mosques in North America, and during the last two decades a few Muslim social service organizations have also sprung up. The next stage, however, is the establishment of community centres, seniors' centres, and educational institutions. Very few Muslims send their children to Islamic schools, and there are almost no Muslim seminaries or institutes of higher education on this continent. Here, Muslims have spoken admiringly of both Catholics and Jews, who have been able to create and maintain significant medical, educational, and cultural institutions in North America.

How Christians can learn from Muslims

Smith emphasized that faith was a personal matter. This is the heart of interfaith dialogue, because institutions and organizations do not dialogue – people do. Transformed relationships and understanding come from the discussions that take place between people. The first step towards learning about Islam, then, is not to pick up the Qur'an and begin reading, or to observe prayer at a mosque. One starts by finding a Muslim friend with whom to speak.

In large communities this is not a problem, since most everyone is in some kind of contact with Muslims. In smaller or more homogeneous communities, the range of options are admittedly more limited, but it is surprising how many mosques and informal Muslim associations exist outside the main urban centres. One's dialogue partner may be a neighbour, a doctor at the local hospital, a teacher, a restaurant owner, a university professor, a cab driver, a factory worker, a motel owner, or the manager of an ethnic grocery store. Sometimes one can make an acquaintance by working alongside people of other traditions in social justice or service projects such food banks, blood drives, or other charitable causes.

Upon finding a dialogue partner, the second step is to "empty one's cup." This phrase comes from a story from the Zen Buddhist tradition, about a man who thought he knew about Zen and went to visit a famous Zen master. As they began conversing, it became apparent to the master that the man did not want to learn from him, but instead wanted to show off his own knowledge. The master began to serve tea to his guest, but kept pouring after the cup was full, causing the tea to spill over the tray and onto the floor. After a few seconds of this, the man implored the master to stop pouring. The master stopped pouring, then asked the man how he could learn if he first did not empty his cup.

The story teaches that one should come to dialogue with humility, genuinely wanting to learn something from the other person. One also should not attempt to impress upon their partner everything they already know (or think they know). The "empty cup" metaphor suggests several other principles in relating to Muslims. First, one should not begin with difficult questions, since this may be perceived as being offensive or hostile. An obvious example would be a Christian who begins a conversation with a Jew by asking, "So why did your ancestors have Jesus crucified?" Similarly with Muslims, one should not begin by asking questions such as "Why do Muslims hate us?" We may ask difficult questions, but only after we have established a respectful relationship and are fully aware of the power dynamics within that relationship.

Unfortunately, this point is not obvious to many people. I was recently asked to give a lecture to a group about contemporary interpretations of Islam in North America. The question and answer that followed had nothing to do with my talk, but everything to do with prejudices that people had about Muslims. I was asked why the Qur'an was a book of violence, why Muslims were intolerant of non-Muslims, and why Muslims had not condemned terrorism. The fact that this conversation took place five years after the terrorist attacks of 9-11 saddened me; I expected the level of ignorance to have diminished since then.

Second, one should be aware of the sources of information about Islam and the lives of Muslims. Does the information come from contact with actual Muslims and things that they have written? Or does it come from people who have little first-hand information about Islam and Muslims? I am amazed at the number of people whose only information about Islam comes from talk radio, tabloid newspapers, commercial television, or literature by opponents of Islam. It disturbs me how many people trust accounts by former Muslims as being able to represent the truth about Islam. In 2006, for example, a psychiatrist from Syria, now living in Los Angeles, gained attention for interviews in which she disparaged Islam and explained why she was no longer a Muslim. This is not to say that there is no value in reading such accounts, but they do not explain why so many other people choose to remain Muslim.

Third, one should not come to dialogue assuming the worst of the partner's community. The very fact that someone chooses to dialogue with another shows that they have some commitment to learning, and are therefore not bad people. One should not expect, for example, that a Muslim dialogue partner should share blame for evils that some other Muslims may have committed. After the terrorist attacks of 9-11, I was asked repeatedly why Muslims hated America, a question which ignored the reality of the millions of Muslims in the United States who, like me, came to America precisely because they loved it.

Fourth, one should be aware of both the ideals and the realities of the Muslim world. A line from Professor Smith that I add to the syllabus of my world religions course says it well: "Normally persons talk about other people's religions as they are, and about their own as it ought to be." In other words, we tend to overlook areas where our own religion does not live up to its ideals, while at the same time not excusing similar realities in the other religion. We may even interpret horrible abuses of the other religion to be a reflection of its ideals.

Here is one example of how this duplicity works in Christian-Muslim relationships: Christians opposed to abortion know that other Christians who kill abortion doctors are violent extremists, unrepresentative of the majority of Christians. Yet those same Christians may think that all Muslims rejoice in the violence and terror committed by other Muslims. Imagine the parallel in reverse: What if Muslims held the actions of the Ku Klux Klan, the Aryan Brotherhood, or the Nazi party to be representative of the ideals of Christianity?

Finally, after establishing a foundation of friendship, Christians can move on to the next phase of interfaith dialogue: a broader engagement with Muslim culture. It could mean listening to Muslim music, whether songs in praise of the Prophet, or popular music from any part of the Muslim world. It may mean watching films that Muslims have made, in cultures as diverse as Iran, Egypt, Pakistan, and the United States. (A wonderful documentary is *Muhammad: Legacy of a Prophet*, which tells how North American Muslims understand the role of the Prophet in their lives.) Books about Muslim lives (see "Suggestions for Further Reading" on page 218) often give sensitive portrayals of what it means to be a Muslim. Finally, one should also seek out the Muslim art that is available locally, whether it be in a museum or in someone's home. One can appreciate all these cultural treasures, of course, without a dialogue partner – but to properly understand the broader culture, one should discuss them with people steeped in the culture. Reading the Qur'an itself should be the last stage in this journey of dialogue. Through relationships with Muslims, one will have a forum to discuss the ideas and events that the Qur'an touches upon, thus making it less likely that one's reading will be skewed. I would suggest starting with the first chapter and then the last 30 chapters rather than reading the chapters in order. If one wants narrative, then one should read the story of Joseph in Chapter Twelve. If one wants to learn about Muslim views of Jesus and Mary, then one should start with Chapter Nineteen.

The etiquette of hospitality

If you have established a respectful relationship with a Muslim neighbour, then you are ready to invite him or her into your home. Ask about diet concerns beforehand, just as you might ask other guests about food allergies they might have. Muslims are prohibited from eating pork as well as pork products, so you will need to check the ingredients used in recipes. Is there ham in the split pea soup? Are the pierogi fried with bacon? Is there lard in the pie crust? For strict Muslims who follow halal dietary laws, you may buy your meat from a halal butcher, use kosher meat, or else choose a fish or vegetarian option. Muslims are also prohibited from drinking alcohol, so unless you know that your Muslim guest drinks in violation of religious law, have other beverages available.

You should likewise be invited into your Muslim neighbour's home. If not, you might drop gentle hints that you would appreciate such an invitation. Depending on your neighbour's native culture, you may be asked to take off your shoes as you enter their home. Doing so without being asked is a considerate gesture. If you want to bring a gift, bring flowers or a fruit basket. Whether you are a man or a woman, dress modestly. This does not mean women should cover their hair, but neither should they wear miniskirts. Also be aware that some conservative Muslims may not shake hands with people of the opposite sex.

Sharing worship experiences

As the friendship matures, you may ask your friend to take you to a mosque. Do not be surprised if you are not invited to the Friday afternoon service, however, since this is the busiest time of the week for Muslims. At a mosque, dress is important. Men should wear long pants, and shirts that cover their shoulders. A golf shirt is perfectly acceptable, but a tank top would not be. A T-shirt is okay, as long as it does not have an offensive slogan or image on it. Women should wear long pants or ankle-length skirts, and a long sleeved shirt or blouse. They should also bring a scarf to cover their hair.

Regardless of your gender, be prepared to take off your shoes when you arrive at the mosque, which could well have separate entrances for men and women. If you have small children with you they may accompany either parent, but school-age boys should go with the men and girls with the women. Once in the entrance, your host will guide you to the appropriate area in the mosque. There, you can stand or sit and watch the prayers. Once the prayers are performed, some people will leave, while others will remain to perform extra prayers. Other than at the congregational Eid prayers, there is no formal collection as there usually is in a Christian service; but you might bring some cash in case there is a donation box at the door and you would like to contribute.

Next, you might want to invite your Muslim neighbour to your church service. Be sure to explain each part of the order of service, and what is expected of people during these parts, like when to sit and when to stand. Indicate where he or she may participate (singing hymns, for example), and where participation would not be appropriate (taking communion). Let them know what happens during the collection; indicate that as a guest they need not feel obligated to contribute. Of course, be sure to introduce them to people after the service, especially if there is a social hour.

Beyond visiting each other's places of worship, your friendship might extend to planning or participating in an interfaith service. But remember that an interfaith service is different from a Christian service to which Muslims are invited. An interfaith service is a shared experience that respects all of the religious traditions present, so it may take place in a fellowship hall or dining area (in a church or a mosque) rather than in the sanctuary. Symbolically, this shows that your goal is not to convert each other but to share your worship experiences.

Finally, you might want to cultivate further dialogue in your congregational context. While having a Muslim speak at your church once is good, it is even better to have Muslims visit over a longer period of time. I have taught several week-long courses on Islam and interfaith dialogue in British Columbia, at the Naramata Centre of the United Church of Canada. This has allowed us to discuss faith in much more detail than during any one visit to a church. It was at Naramata that I became friends with Jim and Jean Strathdee, and have visited with them several times at their home church, St. Mark's United Methodist Church in Sacramento, where they are the music directors. Not only have I worshipped with them, but I have also been welcomed into the homes of several families from their congregation.

Of course, these events can take place among people of other faiths as well. I think of a wonderful experience with Rabbi James Kaufman and his Reform congregation of Valley Beth Hillel in the San Fernando Valley where I live. After an interfaith meeting in which we had both participated, he invited me to come to his congregation over two consecutive Sabbaths, and we both spoke to the congregation. He then arranged a five-week study group about Islam. The multiple sessions allowed us to talk about the serious issues of peace and violence, women's roles, and the Israeli/Palestinian conflict. We could only do that in a meaningful way over time, not in any one presentation to his congregation.

A path of reconciliation

I close this book with a brief reflection on some words that Wilfred Cantwell Smith wrote in 1977: "The religious history of the world is the history of *us*. Some of us have been Muslims, some Christians. Our common history has been what it has been, in significant part because of this fact. Yet it is a common history for all that; and cannot be properly understood otherwise." Muslims and Christians have been in each other's lives since the seventh century. We did not develop in isolation from each other, as did aboriginal communities of Canada and Australia. Rather, we share a common history and a common civilization.

In this book I have tried to emphasize the commonality between our two faith traditions, the two largest in the world. The emerging paradigm of Christianity is leading more and more Christians to explore these commonalities. In fact, some contemporary Christians find they have more in common with some Muslims than they do with more traditional fellow-Christians.

There are profound differences, to be sure, which is precisely why both Muslims and Christians need to understand their histories. North American Muslims already know a great deal about European and North American histories by virtue of their education on this continent, but they also need to learn about Christianity. It may be even more pressing for North American

Christians, who are the majority, to learn about Islam. In the past, their main stance toward Muslims has been as colonizers or missionaries beyond their own shores. Today, Muslims are their neighbours. Some Christians on this continent continue to seek to convert Muslims, and some Muslims likewise seek to convert Christians. Neither of these options will make for peace between our communities. It is only in understanding our history, and particularly the harm that we have done to each other, that we can move forward.

I hope that this book is one signpost on the path of reconciliation that lies before us. We must choose to walk that path together; we have no other choice. As Muslims and as Christians, we are called to a common future based on our common heritage. We both hear the call from God to transform our lives. If we really believe that we have obligations to the one true God, then we will recognize that we have obligations to each other as well. God's peace and blessing are meant to be shared equally among all of God's children.

Endnotes

Foreword

[1] Derek Evans formerly served as Deputy Secretary General of Amnesty International and as Executive Director of the Naramata Centre for Continuing Education. He is an Associate of the Wosk Centre for Dialogue at Simon Fraser University. His most recent book is *Before the War* (Northstone, 2004). As the United Church of Canada's McGeachy Senior Scholar for 2005–2006, he is currently working on a book entitled *Practicing Reconciliation*.

[2] *The Economist*, February 11, 2006 (vol. 378, No. 8464).

Chapter 2: Who are the Muslims?

[1] A longer version of this was published in my PhD dissertation, "The Canadian Face of Islam: Muslim Communities in Toronto," (Centre for the Study of Religion, University of Toronto, 2001).

[2] For a fascinating presentation of that story, see Maria Rosa Menocal's *Shards of Love: Exile and the Origins of the Lyric* (Durham: Duke University Press, 1994).

Chapter 3: Muhammad: the Beloved Prophet

[1] I choose not to give the paper further publicity by naming it.

[2] Translated by Michael Sells, a professor at the University of Chicago, and recognized as the best American translator of the Qur'an. Taken from his book, *Approaching the Qur'an: The Early Revelations* (Ashland, Oregon: White Cloud Press, 1999).

[3] See Asin's *Islam and the Divine Comedy* (Delhi, India: Goodword Books, 2001).

Chapter 4: The Qur'an: the Ultimate Revelation

[1] Michael Sells' magisterial book *Approaching the Qur'an: The Early Revelations*, does this for newcomers to the Qur'an. Sells translates only the opening and the last 30 chapters of the text, and provides a CD with recitations of some of these chapters.

Chapter 5: Surrender to God: Muslim Faith and Life

[1] Canadian Muslim filmmaker Zarqa Nawaz has directed a documentary about her experiences with gender segregation in mosques, entitled *Me and the Mosque*. The film was produced by Joe MacDonald for the National Film Board of Canada, and is available through the NFB.

Chapter 7: Roles of women and men

[1] One important group doing this work in the modern world is Karamah: Muslim Women Lawyers for Human Rights. Their work can be found at: www.karamah.org.

[2] *The Muslim Veil in North America*, edited by Sajida Alvi, Homa Hoodfar, and Sheila McDonough is an excellent resource for those interested in the complexities of why some Muslim women wear the veil, while others do not.

[3] One of my personal favourite hadiths concerns a man who asked the Prophet who he should honour most among all people. Muhammad responded, "Your mother." The man asked, "And after her, whom?" The Prophet responded, "Your mother." The man replied, "And after her, whom?" The Prophet said, "Your mother, and after her, your father."

Chapter 9: From tolerance to dialogue

[1] The document and accompanying study guide can be freely downloaded from http://www.united-church.ca/twmkeo/

Suggestions for further reading

Websites

www.uga.edu/islam
The best website for the academic study of Islam. Created by Professor Alan Godlas at the University of Georgia, it includes substantial links to any major topic of interest about Islam.

www.usc.edu/dept/MSA
Maintained by the Muslim Students Association at the University of Southern California, this site has useful links about Islam, as well as a comprehensive search index of the Qur'an and the hadith literature. The Qur'an page also gives the texts of three different English translations of the Qur'an.

www.karamah.org
Karamah: Muslim Women Lawyers for Human Rights offers information about Islamic law and women.

www.law.emory.edu/IHR/index.html
In several languages, the Islam and Human Rights project at Emory University in Georgia lists information about resources on Islam and human rights.

www.zakariya.net
The web page of Mohamed Zakariya, the finest Muslim calligrapher in North America. An excellent resource for learning about his work, as well as more generally about Islamic calligraphy.

www.lacma.org/islamic_art/islamic.htm
A wonderful resource about the history of Islamic art, maintained by the Los Angeles County Museum of Art.

www.muslimphilosophy.com
An excellent site for the study of Islamic philosophy. It includes numerous links to pages about particular Muslim philosophers.

Books

Abou El Fadl, Khaled. *The Great Theft: Wrestling Islam from the Extremists.* New York: HarperCollins, 2005. A top North American scholar of Islamic law looks at the difference between extremist and moderate Muslims, and helps moderate Muslims to reclaim Islam.

Alvi, Sajida Sultana, Homa Hoodfar, and Sheila McDonough, eds. *The Muslim Veil in North America: Issues and Debates.* Toronto: Women's Press, 2003. A good collection of essays about the issues of hijab in Canada.

Arkoun, Mohammed, translated by Robert Lee. *Rethinking Islam: Common Questions, Uncommon Answers.* Boulder: Westview Press, 1994. This short book by one of the most respected scholars of the Qur'an answers a number of important questions about Islam.

Asin, Miguel. *Islam and the Divine Comedy.* Delhi: Goodword Books, 2001. A Spanish scholar's investigation into the relationships between the accounts of Muhammad's ascent to heaven and Dante's classic.

Blair, Sheila and Jonathan Bloom, eds. *The Art and Architecture of Islam 1250 – 1800.* New Haven: Yale University Press, 1996. A wonderful introduction to later Islamic art – a companion to the volume on early Islamic art described below.

Borg, Marcus J. *The Heart of Christianity: Rediscovering a Life of Faith.* New York: HarperCollins, 2003. An introduction to the earlier and emerging paradigms of Christianity.

Bulliet, Richard W. *The Case for Islamo-Christian Civilization.* New York: Columbia University Press, 2004. An eminent historian of the Middle East makes the case for a shared civilization between Christians and Muslims.

Chamberlin, J. Edward. *If This is Your Land, Where are Your Stories? Finding Common Ground.* Toronto: Vintage Canada, 2004. An English professor writes about the power of stories.

Chittick, William C. *The Sufi Doctrine of Rumi, Illustrated Edition.* Bloomington:World Wisdom, 2005. An excellent introduction to the ideas of the great Sufi master Jalal al-Din Rumi. The author is a top scholar of Sufism in North America and the best translator of Rumi. The many illustrations add to the value of this small volume.

Daniel, Norman. *Islam and the West: The Making of an Image.* Oxford: Oneworld Publications, 2000. The classic study of the development of Western attitudes to Islam and Muslims.

Esposito, John. *The Islamic Threat, Myth or Reality?*, third edition. New York: Oxford University Press, 1999. A guide to political Islam in the contemporary world.

Esposito, John., ed. *The Oxford Encyclopedia of the Modern Islamic World.* New York: Oxford University Press, 1995. A wonderful four-volume resource for those interested in issues of contemporary Islam.

Ettinghausen, Richard, Oleg Grabar and Marilyn Jenkins-Madina, eds. *Islamic Art and Architecture 650–1250,* second edition. New Haven: Yale University Press, 2003. An excellent introduction to early Islamic art, companion to Blair and Bloom's work, cited above.

Fakhry, Majid. *A History of Islamic Philosophy,* third edition. New York: Columbia University Press, 2004. The standard scholarly introduction to Islamic philosophy.

Gibb, Camilla. *Sweetness in the Belly.* Toronto: Doubleday Canada, 2005. This magical yet sensitive novel depicts Muslim life in Ethiopia and in Ethiopian communities in London.

Haddad, Yvonne Y., and Jane I. Smith, eds. *Muslim Communities in North America.* Albany: State University of New York Press, 1994. A good introduction to the ways in which Muslims construct their religious identities in North America.

Hart, Michael. *The 100: A Ranking of the Most Influential Persons in History.* New York: Citadel Press, 1992. This book ranks the Prophet Muhammad first as the most influential person in history.

Khalidi, Tarif. *The Muslim Jesus: Sayings and Stories in Islamic Literature.* Cambridge: Harvard University Press, 2001. A noted scholar of Arabic collects and translates more than 300 Muslim sayings about Jesus.

LeVine, Mark. *Why They Don't Hate Us: Lifting the Veil on the Axis of Evil.* Oxford: Oneworld Publications, 2005. A young historian and musician examines historical and political issues of Muslims in their relationship to the West, particularly through music.

Lings, Martin. *Muhammad: His Life Based on the Earliest Sources.* Vermont: Inner Traditions, 2005. The best biography of the Prophet written from the perspective of a believing Muslim from within the Sunni tradition. It gives the reader a flavour of the traditional Arabic biographies of the Prophet.

Mamdani, Mahmood. *Good Muslim, Bad Muslim: America, the Cold War, and the Roots of Terror.* New York: Pantheon Books, 2004. An account of the complicated relationships between the American government and the Muslim world during the arming of the Afghan mujahideen.

McAuliffe, Jane, ed. *The Encyclopaedia of the Qur'an.* Leiden: E.J. Brill, 2001–2005. This magnificent five volume collection is the standard English language reference work on the Qur'an.

Menocal, María Rosa. *The Arabic Role in Medieval Literary History: A Forgotten Heritage.* Philadelphia: University of Pennsylvania Press, 2004. This brilliant work shows the shared literary history of Jewish, Christian and Muslim traditions, particularly in Spain.

Menocal, María Rosa. *Shards of Love: Exile and the Origins of the Lyric.* Durham: Duke University Press, 1994. Beginning with an account of how crucial elements were left out of the story of Columbus's voyage to America, Menocal describes the interweaving of Jewish, Muslim and Christian contributions to medieval European culture.

Mottahedeh, Roy. *The Mantle of the Prophet: Religion and Politics in Iran,* second edition. Oxford: Oneworld Publications, 2002. One of the best single volumes on events leading up to the revolution in Iran.

Murata, Sachiko, and William C. Chittick. *The Vision of Islam.* New York: Paragon House, 1994. The two specialists on Islam provide an excellent introduction to Islamic theology.

Oxtoby, Willard G. *The Meaning of Other Faiths.* Philadelphia: Westminster Press, 1983. A Presbyterian minister and scholar of comparative religion examines how Christians can understand other religious traditions.

Peters, Francis E. *Muhammad and the Origins of Islam.* Albany: State University of New York Press, 1994. The best critical biography of Muhammad, written by a distinguished secular historian.

Postman, Neil, and Steve Powers. *How to Watch TV News.* New York: Penguin Books, 1992. A short guide to the inner workings of network television news, written by a scholar of media and a practicing journalist.

Qureshi, Emran and Michael A. Sells, eds. *The New Crusades: Constructing the Muslim Enemy.* New York: Columbia University Press, 2003. An excellent collection of essays on the representations of Islam and Muslim lives.

Rushdie, Salman. *Imaginary Homelands: Essays and Criticism 1981 – 1991.* London: Granta Books, 1991. A collection of Rushdie's essays and reviews, including a number of essays about racism in Britain. An excellent introduction to his non-fiction.

Safi, Omid, ed. *Progressive Muslims: On Justice, Gender and Pluralism.* Oxford: Oneworld Publications, 2003. A collection of essays by Muslim scholars of Islam on these contemporary topics.

Schimmel, Annemarie. *Mystical Dimensions of Islam.* Chapel Hill: University of North Carolina Press, 1975. The standard introduction to Sufism by one of its most respected Western interpreters.

Sells, Michael. *Approaching the Qur'an: The Early Revelations.* Oregon: White Cloud Press, 1999. This wonderful translation of the last 30 chapters of the Qur'an comes with a compact disc of different styles of Qur'anic recitation.

Smith, Wilfred Cantwell. *The Meaning and End of Religion,* reprint edition. Minneapolis: Fortress Press, 1991. Perhaps Smith's most important work, this book looks at the use of the term religion, distinguishing between "faith" and "the cumulative tradition."

Index